W9-BMZ-883

To Seekers Everywhere

CONTENTS

INTRODUCTION
(to the 1996 edition)

Before his death on December 20, 1994, Elton Trueblood had lived every day of the twentieth century. He was born on December 12, 1900, in a farming community of southern Iowa, and was reared in a strict Quaker home where "going to Meeting" was as much a part of life as eating or sleeping. The disciplined atmosphere of his growing years provided a strong foundation for his career as a college professor and Christian author, since the living of a disciplined life was the basis for his pursuit of excellence in both teaching and writing. In his autobiography, *While It Is Day*, he described how the Christian Endeavor Society of the local Friends church helped him to undertake his first voluntary discipline:

> I signed the pledge to take some part, other than singing, in every meeting of the Society, and also to engage daily in both Bible reading and prayer. Honoring my signature, I kept the promise, thus early learning something of the power released by the voluntary acceptance of discipline...[1]

Besides learning the value of discipline, Elton Trueblood's Quaker upbringing implanted within him an understanding of Christianity that affected the whole of his adult life, and influenced every major

---

[1] Elton Trueblood, *While It Is Day*, (New York: Harper and Row, 1974), p. 15.

piece of his writing. He was taught at an early age that the essence of Quakerism is merely the attempt to exemplify the basic Christian faith. He believed, as did William Penn, that Quakerism is simply "Christianity writ plain," and a careful study of Trueblood's writings will show that his career was devoted to helping people go beyond the ceremonies and symbols of any ritualistic faith, to this basic understanding of essential Christianity. He was convinced that, by carefully studying the faith of the New Testament, the contemporary church will, in turn, be revived, since Christians can thus judge their mild religion by the dynamic faith of the Early Church. To be as much like Christ as we can is the Christian's goal, and if this goal is to be realized, the believer must understand the basics of his or her faith. The writings of Elton Trueblood help to point the seeker to the vitality of the Christian message, thus encouraging him or her to become a finder.

One of the curious observations to be made in these, the closing years of the century, is that many people are discovering that the danger Elton Trueblood foretold over fifty years ago is now a frightening reality. The "cut-flower" civilization, which he described in his book, *The Predicament of Modern Man,* in 1944, is now coming to pass. The words which we find most prophetic, and which strike at the heart of our current crisis, are as follows:

> The terrible danger of our time consists in the fact that ours is a cut-flower civilization. Beautiful as cut flowers may be, and much as we may use our ingenuity to keep them looking fresh for a while, they will eventually die, and they die because they are severed from their sustaining roots. We are trying to maintain the dignity of the individual apart from the deep faith that every person is made in God's image and is therefore precious in God's eyes...[2]

[2] Elton Trueblood, *The Predicament Of Modern Man,* (New York: Harper and Row, 1994), p. 59.

With these words Trueblood guides his readers to the heart of our human predicament. We are a society trying to live in the dungeon of subjectivity, cut off from the living God, and, as a result, the current generation often denies even the existence of any objective moral order. "What we need," he continues, "is not an assertion of our own ideals, but contact with the eternally real... What person's need, if they are to overcome their lethargy and weakness, is some contact with the real world in which moral values are centered in the nature of things. This is the love of God, for which persons have long shown themselves willing to live or to die. The only sure way in which we can transcend our human relativities is by obedience to the absolute and eternal God."[3]

Elton Trueblood boldly proclaimed himself an "Evangelical Christian." He considered a "non-evangelical Christian" a contradiction in terms. He came to this understanding of the faith after a great deal of study, and particularly following his reading of C.S. Lewis. In his early ministry Trueblood often mentioned Christ in his messages and writings, but he did not emphasize his uniqueness. It was C.S. Lewis who finally "shocked" him out of his unexamined liberalism. "In reading Lewis," he wrote, "I could not escape the conclusion that the popular view of Christ as being a teacher, and only a teacher, has within it a self-contradiction that cannot be resolved. I saw, in short, that conventional liberalism cannot survive rigorous and rational analysis. What Lewis and a few others made me face was the hard fact that if Christ was only a teacher, then he was a false one, since, in his teaching, he claimed to be more."[4]

There were a number of outstanding aspects of the Trueblood personality that should be examined in this brief introduction, and will prove to be helpful to the reader as he or she begins the pilgrimage through this life of search. We must begin by asking the question of

[3] *The Predicament Of Modern Man*, pp. 60-61.
[4] *While It Is Day*, p. 99.

why Elton Trueblood stood as a giant in the field of religious writing and thinking. What was the secret of his highly successful career as an author, teacher, and minister-at-large? This question is not easily answered, but we can begin to understand the greatness of the Trueblood personality when we look at a combination of factors working in conjunction with one another, rather than as isolated elements.

The first recognizable quality of genuine magnitude is discipline, a quality, as mentioned before, that was developed at a very young age. Elton Trueblood was the most disciplined man I have ever known. He discovered the rewards of self-discipline, since he knew full well that inherent in the human race is the tendency toward laziness, which, if left unchecked, becomes sinful waste. He regarded time as a sacred gift, and used every minute of every day as a witness to the glory of God. He was a very structured individual who maintained a schedule that would have exhausted persons half his age.

Coupled with this strict discipline was his availability to students. His very structured life and his openness to the possibility of change, if he was needed somewhere else, might at first seem to be contradictory. But, upon further evaluation, one can see that they are complementary. Trueblood's discipline enabled him to have time for those who needed his help. Hard at work on a manuscript or a speech, I have seen him put all of that work aside and devote his undivided attention to a student who was having difficulty in his or her studies. He always found time to help anyone who came to his door.

Another very important aspect of the Trueblood profile was his devotion to academic excellence. He was unswerving in his dedication to the development of the mind. His own career as an academician took him through the halls of Harvard and Johns Hopkins. Under the tutelage of the famous Arthur O. Lovejoy of Johns Hopkins, and Willard L. Sperry of Harvard, Elton Trueblood acquired a deep appreciation for hard, disciplined study. Those of us who were his students were especially aware of this important aspect of emphasis. This concern was given expression in his essay on "The Redemption of the College," where he pleaded for a new reformation on the campuses of Christian schools:

> Part of our purpose is the production of Christian in-
> tellectuals, men and women who can combine the love of
> God with the love of learning. If this is not done in the way of
> excellence, it will not be done at all. The option provided by
> the existence of the Christian college should be harder rather
> than easier, when compared with its alternatives, for we are
> in a more ambitious enterprise than are our competitors.
> This, however, is something which we have sometimes failed
> to realize, but unless we recognize it, we shall not survive
> and furthermore, we shall not deserve to survive.[5]

Always he was pushing Christians toward the standards of excellence, striving to equip them for the hard task of defending their faith in the midst of the arrogant paganism that infects our age. He was a Christian encourager, and took for his golden text the words of St. Paul found in I Thessalonians 5:11, "Therefore encourage one another, and build one another up." (RSV) One of the best examples of Trueblood's fulfilling this command of Paul was found in the way he encouraged students of all ages to excel.

Coupled with this demand for scholarly achievement was Elton Trueblood's sensitivity and openness in the worship of God. For him, intellectualism did not necessarily mean dull formalism, since he believed and demonstrated that clear, hard thinking can be combined with a warm, worshipful heart. Thus, he felt equally comfortable in the midst of a philosophical or theological debate,

---

[5] Elizabeth Newby, *A Philosopher's Way: Essays and Addresses of Elton Trueblood*, (Nashville: Broadman Press, 1978), p. 123.

or singing, "Jesus, Lover of My Soul" in a village service of worship. The intellectual dimension of the Christian faith, he insisted, did not have to be separated from a meaningful Christ-centered experience of reverence. Thinking and feeling in the religious life was a combination that Elton Trueblood consciously sought to keep in balance.

One more combination in the Trueblood personality should be noted: Although he was a serious, philosophical thinker and teacher, he had a penetrating sense of humor. While he realized the tragedy of so much of our human predicament, and sought through the medium of logical thinking to help people better to understand this often difficult and complicated life, he never lost his perspective and was always ready to hear or share a funny story. Humor, he felt, provided meaningful interludes in the continuous process of rigorous thinking. He often used the quotation from Abraham Lincoln, who when asked one day why he was always laughing, responded in characteristic Lincoln style, "If I did not laugh, I would cry." Elton Trueblood made Abraham Lincoln one of his most influential models, and wrote an important book concerning the Great Emancipator, entitled, *Abraham Lincoln: Theologian of American Anguish.* Nowhere does the similarity of these two men become more apparent than in the way they have faced both the triumphs and tragedies of life, combining a sense of serious concern with a humorous disposition.

In the style of Samuel Johnson, another of Trueblood's models, he was a devout moralist. Although his writing was prophetic, always warning his readers about their condition and the condition of the world, it also inspired reassurance and trust. Hence, for the past fifty years, those who have been reading Elton Trueblood have not only been led to adjust their thinking in a logical way, but they have also experienced a sense of relief in the hope of redemption. I believe this to be the greatest single reason why Elton Trueblood's writing has remained so popular for so many years, and is the way in which his conjunct life was best expressed. He was honest with his public concerning the dire predicament of our time, but, along with this note of prophetic insight, the reader was always lifted by a resounding sense of hope.

In this literary style Elton Trueblood had no rival. His ability to capture the human situation, and then to call on Christians to move from complacency to commitment in making a response, while, at the same time, helping us to develop a sustaining trust and hope in Jesus Christ, was the work of a special kind of genius. Where most religious authors are tempted to isolate the pessimistic side of human existence, with little or no regard given to the bright spots, or to create a false trust in an empty optimism that does not mention the darker aspects of life, Elton Trueblood combined an emphasis upon both. Because he appreciated the necessity of paradox, his writing is both disturbing and refreshing at the same time. He cut through the bleakness of contemporary decay to the essentials of Christian hope, while keeping steadily in mind the problems of decay. This combination of optimism and pessimism, realism and idealism, made Elton Trueblood unique in his field.

Elton Trueblood, who, before his death was considered the dean of American religious writers, was one of the most prolific authors of the twentieth century. Thirty-six volumes, countless articles, and numerous lectures have been the products of his pen. This man who was deeply concerned about human life chose the discipline of writing to record these concerns and insights into the human situation. His writing has not been primarily for the academic. He wrote, instead, for the committed Christian seeker who needs a plan to follow, and an encouraging word for a depressed spirit. The concerns about which Elton Trueblood wrote have been nourished in the belief that Christians are called to be participants and not mere spectators, to be actively working from a Christian perspective toward solutions to the problems of our world, and not just bench warmers on the sidelines. He does not offer his readers words that only comfort them; he gives them a challenge from which they cannot easily turn away.

In the June 1994 Quarterly Yoke Letter, Elton Trueblood wrote: "At the age of ninety-three I am well aware that I do not have many years left... How do I want to be remembered? Not primarily as a Christian scholar, but rather as a loving person. This can be the goal of every individual. If I can be remembered as a truly loving person I shall be satisfied."

Little did we know at the time that this would be Trueblood's last writing for publication, and that he would be leaving this earthly life within seven short months. He died in his sleep on the evening of December 20, 1994, eight days into his ninety-fifth year.

As early as 1957 this concern for being remembered as a loving person was noted in his diary. "For many years I have been conscious of a tension in my life," Elton wrote. "On the one hand I felt the need, with strict loyalty to logical consistency, to explore erroneous and shoddy thinking, particularly among students. On the other hand I have felt the demands of compassion for these same persons. The difficulty is that loyalty to the former conception sometimes gives the impression that the latter is lacking. In some cases it seems necessary to choose, because insistence on logical rigor will have at least the appearance of lack of love.

"Now nearly fifty-seven years of age, I have determined that in the remainder of my life, I shall try to err, if I err, on the side of tenderness. Perhaps I have done the service required of one in maintaining sharpness of mind, and my future role is that of being obviously loving as well as really loving. At least the experiment is worth trying."

As one studies the life of Elton Trueblood, this shift of emphasis is detectable. Although he never abandoned his strong concern for clear thinking and logical rigor, he did, as he grew into a time of remembrance and gratitude, make the move toward combining this concern with the "warm heart." This shift was noticeable in his writing, but in his speaking and personal encounters the move was most discernible. In reading the early sermons Trueblood delivered (for example, "The New Apologetics," which was his first sermon at Woonsocket, Rhode Island, Friends Meeting) and then hearing him speak in recent years, one realizes, that he had shifted from complexity of discourse to a profound and loving simplicity. In a recent sermon, he chose as his text I Corinthians 14:1—"Make love your aim." His entire message focused on "caring as the supreme work of persons." He pointed out the fact that love is used forty-seven times in the Gospel of John, twenty as a verb and twenty-seven as a noun. In John's First Letter, he noted love appears twenty-five times. In conclusion he said, "I want to use the time that I have left to care for as many as I can."

This message, which was not simplistic yet profoundly simple, is in stark contrast to the tough thinking and strong debating style that had marked Trueblood's earlier career. In 1957 he had made the decision to err on the side of tenderness and to be more loving, and in the more than thirty-seven years since, one can see how this tenderness of concern grew. What made his care and loving concern for persons so meaningful was the fact that he had come to this place through the fire of tough-mindedness and impatience for sloth. The simplicity of his message of love and caring would not have been nearly as profound had he not struggled long and hard with tough and complex philosophical questions. I am reminded of the question asked of the theologian Karl Barth toward the end of his life, concerning the one truth he would like to share with others. His response: "Jesus loves me this I know, for the Bible tells me so." Perhaps a profound simplicity is the fruit of arduous study that passes through the maze of complex thought. This seems to be the case in the life of Elton Trueblood, as well as in the life of Karl Barth.

In Plato's *Republic* we read about a conversation between Socrates and Cephalus. Socrates is reported as saying, "There is nothing which for my part I like better, Cephalus, than conversing with aged men; for I regard them as travelers who have gone on a journey which I too may have to go, and of whom I ought to inquire whether the way is smooth and easy, or rugged and difficult....Is life harder towards the end?" The old man replied to the inquiry of Socrates by saying, "Old age has a great sense of calm and freedom."

I became Elton Trueblood's associate in 1979, when he was seventy-eight years old. I can attest, as will many others, that in the last chapter of his life he did, indeed, experience "a great sense of calm and freedom." I was with him last exactly one month prior to his death, and although he was weak, the sense of calm and freedom was still prevalent. It was obvious that it was becoming increasingly difficult for his physical body to hold his adventurous spirit.

Above the large fireplace in the Earlham College Dining Hall, the following words are inscribed on a long and wide wooden beam. Elton Trueblood was fond of repeating them at each Annual Yokefellow Conference banquet: "They gathered sticks, kindled a fire, and left it burning." It is a direct quotation from the log of Robert Fowler, who was the captain of the Quaker sailing vessel Woodhouse. Before the ship left England for America in the late seventeenth century, it docked on the south of England for repairs. Because repairs took several days, the Quakers on board left the ship to go into the surrounding communities and share the Christian message. In recording what took place, the captain wrote, "The Ministers of Christ were not idle, they gathered sticks, kindled a fire, and left it burning."

Elton Trueblood knew his earthly time was near the end. In the months before his death he spoke with a sense of finality. He was fond of quoting the words of Stephen Grellet: "I expect to pass through this world but once. Any good, therefore, that I can do, or any kindness I can show, let me do it now. Let me not withhold or defer it, for I shall not pass this way again."

Passing this way once is probably enough for Elton. He has kindled many loving fires and left them burning.

It seems appropriate at this point of closure in the earthly life of Elton Trueblood, and at this time in the history of the Christian faith, that this volume be published. In brief, this book is a collection of "Trueblood signposts," hewn from a faith which wore out numerous chisels. Sharing out of a lifetime of study and reflection, and as a committed Christian who firmly believed that "Christians can out-think all opposing philosophies," he writes simply, yet profoundly, about what he learned on his journey. Out of the trustworthiness of his own spiritual experience, interacting with his discipline of logic and his ethic of love, Elton Trueblood places his signposts carefully for those who will follow. Here he shares his thoughts on the most basic of Christian topics—A Reasonable Faith for Today, The Importance of Christ, The Necessity of the Church, A Holistic Faith, and The Future of Christianity. As a prologue Trueblood offers one of the last things he wrote, *Seek and You Will Find...* and as an Epilogue, his dear friend and colleague, Landrum Bolling, shares a tribute. The basis for these "signposts" was a series of lectures delivered in Richmond, Indiana, at the inauguration of the Yokefellow Academy, now Trueblood Academy, and supplemented by previously unpublished Quarterly Yoke Letters.

In the end each seeker must make his or her own way through the maze of questions, absurdities, and incoherent patterns which life brings, validating a belief system by each one's own spiritual experience. Only then does it become a living faith. We can, however, learn from the experiences of those who have gone before us, relating our own experiences to what others have found. We are all so far from the truth that we cannot afford to dismiss the help of others.

So, I am grateful to Elton Trueblood, fellow pilgrim and spiritual seeker, for the signposts he has left us. He has been an encourager in my own life of search, and I am confident that readers will experience this same source of encouragement. Prepare to be challenged by a master teacher.

James R. Newby
January 1, 1996

PROLOGUE

Seek and You Will Find . . .

In his famous defense against his accusers, a high point is reached when Socrates tells what he expects in life after death. He affirms clearly his conviction that there will be another world, free from the injustices of the present existence. Thus we have in the *Apology*, a clear affirmation of immortal life four centuries before Christ. The greatest joys to be experienced in our future life are those of fellowship with persons from whom we can learn.

Socrates explains his hope by reference to many eminent persons. In short, he has made a list of persons whom he hopes to see: "And above all I should like to spend my time there, as here, in examining and searching people's minds, to find out who is really wise among them, and who only thinks that he is." In short, the heavenly life is pictured as an unending dialogue, in which there is opportunity to ask questions. "What one would not give, gentlemen, to be able to question the leader of that great host against Troy, or Odysseus or Sisyphus, or the thousands of other men and women whom one could mention, to talk and mix and argue with whom would be unimaginable happiness?" In short, Socrates believed that in the life everlasting, he would actually talk with Agamemnon and others like him, and that such happiness would go on forever.

Whether the life, after our human life, will be what is so vividly described by Socrates we cannot know, but we do know that many of our best times in the present life are times of sharing of ideas.

As we learn from one another, the world we inhabit becomes larger. Material things decay, but the spiritual life does not. There is no end to the questions we may reasonably ask.

If the great message of the *Apology* is right, we ought to prepare for life that is truly immortal. You and I can make a list of those whom we expect to meet and from whom we can continue to learn. I have long had such a list. At the top of my list is Christ himself. The Gospels are priceless, but they give us only a small portion of Christ's teaching. He told us to be Seekers, and this command I expect to try to obey.

As a Quaker, it is important for me to understand that the Quaker movement really began with Seekers. When George Fox stood on the top of Pendle Hill and saw a great people to be gathered, many of them whom he saw were already called Seekers. It would not have been strange if we had adopted this name, rather than the name Friends. We adopted the name Friends partly because of Christ's message found in John 15:15, but we were well aware that we were still trying to learn.

All of our life here on earth is fundamentally a preparation for the life everlasting. We make many mistakes, but we have a few firm beliefs. We can turn, with confidence, to the high point of the teaching of Socrates in the following words: "Fix your minds on this one belief, which is certain—that nothing can harm a good man either in life or after death."

There were brave men before Agamemnon, and there were wise men before Socrates, but we shall ask them many questions. In all real religions there is an element of search, and the search never ends. Our life here on earth is only the beginning of life eternal.

If any one thinks that he has wisdom, the one sure truth is that he does not. The more we advance, the more clear it is that we still have a long way to go.

We are close to the heart of the Gospel when we study the passage about searching. We have the words in both Matthew and Luke, and we can never turn to them often enough. The version in Luke is as follows:

> And I tell you, ask and it will be given you; seek and you will find, knock and it will be opened to you. For everyone who asks receives, and he who seeks finds, and to him who knocks it will be opened. (Luke 11:9)

D. Elton Trueblood

Though reason is necessary to the Christian faith, it is probable that most people are not, in fact, drawn to a full faith by intellectual arguments. *Can you by searching find out God?* (Job 11:7) is still a question to which the answer is presumably negative. But if we end at this point we are missing important elements of practical significance. One of the chief of these is that strict honesty in reasoning may help immensely in answering objections to the faith that is centered in Jesus Christ. Though reason alone may not enable persons to find God, it can do wonders in enabling them to surmount serious barriers to the achievement of an examined faith.

D.E.T.

CHAPTER 1

A Reasonable Faith for Today

*It ought to be possible to have both the warm heart
and the clear head...to be both tender-hearted
and tough-minded.*

The Christian is called to think. That is not the only thing we are called to do, but as I look around the world in which I move, I see that we do fairly well with prayer, and we are often personally loving. Our trouble is in the thinking. It is very widely believed in many corners of our society that Christianity is obsolete. Many believe that it just goes on as a kind of vestige of an earlier or pre-scientific age, and that it is not something that can appeal to a full intellectual. This is a very common and utterly false judgment. The Christian, I am convinced, can out-think all opposition, and we are called to do so.

A glorious text for the life of reason is found in I Peter 3:15, "Always be ready to give a reason to anyone who asks you about the hope that is in you, but do it with tenderness and reverence." It isn't enough just to say, "I believe." Your neighbor, your critic, will say, "Why do you believe? What makes you think so?" "If you believe in God, why do you believe in God?" "If you believe in prayer, why do you believe in prayer?" The voices asking such questions are all around us, in the places where we work and where we live.

"Test all things; hold fast that which is good." (I Thessalonians 5:21) These words come from the first little book written in the New Testament. The idea of a reasonable faith is not some late development, but has been an important part of our heritage all the time. When our Lord was asked what is the greatest commandment, he gave two—one about God and one about the neighbor. It is a double priority. First of all, he quoted a passage from Deuteronomy, which is called the Shema. The Shema is repeated today in every Hebrew Synagogue the world over, and so it was in the days of Christ. The way in which Jesus gave it was very striking, because he added the word *mind*. "Thou shall love the Lord thy God with all thy strength, and all thy soul, and all thy mind." And then he added, and, "Thou shall love thy neighbor as thyself."

The second comes from Leviticus. So far as we know this is the first time in the history of the world that these two were brought together in one single context. If you ever doubt the necessity of the life of reason for the Christian, our Lord's words themselves are extremely impressive. This means that faith is not enough. We all have faith. We have to live by faith, of course, but we never live by mere faith. You don't go on having faith in a person who does not keep his or her promises. Mere faith would be the same as superstition.

A student of mine [Elizabeth Newby] has written a book titled, *A Migrant with Hope*. This is a young woman who until she was fourteen years old had never slept under a roof, but in the back of a truck. That is where her mother, father, and brothers lived with her. A tarpaulin was over it to keep off the rain. It was a most primitive kind of life, because her father was a migrant farm worker. He picked the tomatoes of Indiana, hoed the beets of Colorado, picked the cotton of Texas, and so forth. And now she is a cultivated, brilliant woman.

One of the most moving things in her book was the faith of her father in an incantation. As a little girl she contracted some kind of disease of the lungs, perhaps a form of influenza. He took her out where there was a great anthill of red ants, and forced her to jump both ways over the anthill in the shape of a cross. He had faith that that act would cure the influenza. All thinking people can see the absurdity of it. It is mere superstition. It apparently had nothing to do with the situation, but he had faith in it.

Keep that kind of story in mind when you hear people say that faith is enough. What we need is not a mere faith, but a reasonable faith, a faith that has some substantiation in experience, in logic, and in careful scrutiny. The question is never one of saying that faith is bad. Faith is very good and necessary. You can't have a marriage without it, and you can't have a church without it. It must never, however, be merely unthinking faith, but a faith which is substantiated.

We want Christians, then, who are believers, but who know why they are believers. I am a believer. I believe in God. I believe that God is. I believe that God would be if we were not. I believe that God is like Jesus Christ. I believe God is one to whom we can pray, and one who knows about us and is concerned with every individual in the world. It is a very big order, but I believe it. It isn't enough, however, to say that I believe it. I need to be able to substantiate it, to make it part of a coherent world view, and that is what is meant by the life of reason.

In this life of reason one is always open to change. If you once thought that the earth is flat, as a child is likely to think, of course you will not continue to believe in this way. You let the childish belief be changed by experience, observation, and by rationality. Always be ready to change. There is nothing wrong with changing, but there is a great deal wrong with holding onto a position that is unintelligent, unrealistic, or irrational.

Note that the Christian does not claim that God can be proved absolutely. No Christian has ever claimed that, and no Christian has ever claimed that God can be seen with physical eyes; it isn't that simple. We cannot absolutely prove that God is. We cannot absolutely prove that atoms are. We cannot prove any historical event absolutely, because we could always be wrong, and witnesses could be wrong. What we can do, however, is to find a position that makes sense, that brings together the many aspects of experience of which we are aware. This is what the Christian tries to do as he or she thinks. Christians are never afraid of new evidence. They are not afraid of being questioned. In fact Christians gladly accept questioning, because they have a story to tell.

The Christian Strategy

Knowing that committed Christians are a minority in the world, how are we going to operate? Of course we are a minority. I felt this most strongly the summer I was in Russia under Communist rule. The groups of Christians that I was with were about 500,000, but that is a very tiny number compared with Russia's total population. Not only is this true in Russia, it certainly is true in Western Europe, and it is also true in the United States of America. For us to know that committed Christians are a minority is a great strength because then we will not be under any delusions. Where is the mission field? The mission field is everywhere, including the communities in which we live.

Knowing that we are in that position, how will we form our strategy? It is very important not to be merely defensive. Our neighbors may say, "Christianity is obsolete, and meaningless. It has no basis in fact." Then we might have to defend. There are times when we ought to defend, and that is part of what we mean by giving a reason for the faith that is in us. It is much more important, however, for our strategy to take the offensive. We can all see what happens in a world in which the Christian gospel is lost. We can see that when the fine flowers of civilization are severed from their roots they tend to wither and die. This is much of the trouble we see all around us.

Consider the person who upholds atheism. Atheism is very simple; it is the conviction that God is not. The atheist believes that there is no person beyond the finite persons that live; we have the world of matter and that is limited to our solar system, the galaxies, and so forth. They do not feel, they do not know, they do not think, and they have no purposes. And some atheists say, "That's all there is: the world of matter, and finite persons like us." There is no purpose beyond, no ultimate meaning of the universe, and no one to whom to pray. Therefore, of course, prayer would be foolish. If I saw any good reason to think that that was true, I wouldn't pray anymore. I don't need to waste my time or my energy.

If the Christian faith is not true, it is an evil because it wastes effort. If it is not true, we should not build churches. If it is based on delusions, we should not engage in maintaining a fellowship. This is why Christians are looking for any evidence that we can get, pro or con, on all the great subjects. Atheists, however, have made up their minds. They are convinced that in this universe there is not the infinite person to whom we can pray.

This is a very hard position to defend intellectually. The atheist must admit that there are persons who can think, love, and care. We all know this at first hand. We are personal beings, and we are extremely different from anything else that we know in the finite world.

Compare a person with a stone. The stone does not think, nor does it have consciousness, certainly no self-consciousness. The stone does not know it is a stone: it has no purpose, no sense of meaning, and it is essentially passive. The stone cannot have an ideal, and then following the ideal go out and change events. It just is, and it stays where it is until it is moved by something outside of itself. A person is a terrific contrast, though imperfect. We do not claim to be anything else. But we know that we are imperfect, and that we make mistakes, and that we try to change our lives in the light of the mistakes we make. We have purposes and our purposes produce events.

If God is not, then persons have come from an impersonal world. If God is not, then the stream has risen higher than its source. If God is not, then as thinking beings, we have to deny the whole principle of sufficient reason on which we have to operate. If we hear a noise, we say there must be a cause; we don't just think it comes without a cause. If there is a change in the surface of the earth, as in a trembling, we look for a cause and we find an earthquake, a movement of lava, and so forth. If we did not do this we could not possibly have science. All science is based upon the principle of sufficient reason, i.e. the conviction that for every outcome there is cause, and an adequate cause. If God is not, then at this most crucial point this principle is denied. It means that something has come from nothing, or that the event is superior to that from which it came.

In the beginning of rational thinking in the life of Western Civilization, the philosophers of ancient Greece helped us all. One of their most remarkable helps came in the statement, "from nothing, nothing comes." If God is *not* then that is not true. If an impersonal world of rocks, gravitation, and complete unconsciousness could finally produce a thinking person, a loving person, sometimes a caring person, a purposeful being, then this is a very absurd world, indeed. If the world is that absurd, then you have to expect it to be absurd at all points. The whole basis of rational discourse would be undermined. It is not the believer in God who is in intellectual trouble, but the unbeliever. It is not, of course, always easy to believe, and we all know the difficulties. But what Christian thinkers soon discovered was that the unbelief is much more difficult to maintain intellectually. This is important to keep in mind whenever people say that the Christian is just one who is emotional, who only feels, or who engages in wish-thinking. The answer is exactly the opposite:

the Christian is one who can be tough-minded, and he or she can see the difficulties of an alternative position. If the difficulties of the alternative position are greater than that which is held by Christians, they will not take it.

Of course there are difficulties in any position. One will never find a position in which it is all easy, or all simple, because this is not a simple world. It is a very complex world. As one who has tried to be a Christian thinker, however, I have been constantly struck with the fact that we do not have to take a secondary place, or believe that we are the ones who are obsolete. We can take the offensive, and show the difficulties of denying the faith.

The Christian Intellectual

The early Christians had an amazing job. They were surrounded by people who had never heard of Christ, and most of the people had never heard of the books we call the Hebrew Scripture or Old Testament. The New Testament had not been written. In the land of Greece where they made such a great advance, talk about Jesus Christ as the Son of God was extremely strange. How could they get a hearing with no money, no prestige, no college, and no book? But they did, and it has been said of them that the reason they did is that they out-thought as well as outlived all opposition. How did they do that? They pointed out the whole idea of the order of the universe and naturally asked the question, is it reasonable to think that all of this could come of itself, without any thought, without any person, and without any purpose? People began to see that if in their own individual lives thought produces events, it is reasonable to suppose that in the universe as a whole, thought has produced events. And so Christians began to speak of Almighty God as the infinite divine thinker, and the world as the result of God's thinking, and God's purpose.

People in the world today assume that there is a conflict between science and the Christian faith. This is accepted almost without argument. Yet it was Christian thinkers who were the ones who did most of the founding of what we call science. The most vivid example is that of Sir Isaac Newton. Newton's idea was that if you really believed in God, if you really loved God, then that would be a terrific motivation for knowing more about God's world. Newton, therefore, thought to know the laws of motion because he really believed that he was thinking God's thoughts after him. And so in the founding of our modern science it was not uncommon for a great scientist, in making a demonstration or putting on an experiment, to say to his students, let us ask God a question, and find out what the laws of gases are, or find out the exact distance to a star. It is God's truth with which we are dealing. This makes for a very powerful motivation. If you falsify your evidence, that is not merely bad science, it is bad religion! That is denying the reverence for God's creation, which inspires those who really believe that it is God's creation.

A few years ago we celebrated the anniversary of the birth of a man who was professor of science, a minister of the Christian faith, and president of Earlham College in Indiana. His name was Joseph Moore. If you go upstairs in the Lilly Library on the Earlham campus, you will see his desk with the three parts so that he could move from one to the other. He sought to hold all of these aspects of his life in one common unity. Christian intellectuals do not put science over in one compartment, and religion in another. They are forced to hold them together so that their world view is a coherent one. It is this that Christian intellectuals must try to accomplish by their reading, their study, and their thinking.

All professing Christians are called to be Christian intellectuals. That might seem a strange idea. One may say, "I have no degree." Socrates did not have a degree. Jesus did not have a degree. Who cares? The main thing is to use the mind that God has given you to the very fullest extent of which you are capable. Humility here, a false humility, can be extremely harmful. We can say, "I don't have any ability. I don't know how to think about these matters. I leave these things to experts." You cannot leave them to experts! One of the chief reasons why you cannot is that when problems are raised, you don't have time to go get the expert. People will raise their faith problems with you wherever you are.

The Problem of Evil

The problem with evil is that which arises when we ask how it is possible for God to be both loving and powerful, and it can be a major stumbling block to a reasonable faith. For example, a woman whom I have known for a quarter of a century is absolutely filled with cancer. She is a good woman. She has given herself unselfishly to Christian causes all of her life, and now at the age of fifty, to all human appearances, she is going to die. Any thoughtful person is bound to ask, "If God cares, how could this be?" The tendency is to say, either God does not care, or God is not able to make a difference. Either God is lacking in concern, or lacking in power.

In considering such a problem, it is important to understand five brief points:

First, Christ in revealing God to us does not promise easy lives. He does not say he will take away all of our burdens, or pains—certainly his was not taken away. In the Garden he prayed: "Oh Father, if it be Thy will take this cross. Nevertheless, not my will but Thine be done." And he was crucified and he died. This is not the end of the story, but we are making a great start in understanding pain and suffering when we realize the Christian faith is not dependent upon an easy success story, but upon the Cross.

Second, pain, terrible as it is, can be redemptive. There are numerous instances where a person who has suffered, has, as a consequence of this suffering, been able to lift up other people by the quality of life shown in response to the pain. The most effective lives are not those in which everything goes beautifully, where everything is nice and everything is lovely. We know what it is like to sit by the bedside of a person in pain, and we go to cheer that person, but in many cases that person cheers us. And so the second important observation is: even pain, bad as it is, can, under certain circumstances, be redemptive.

Third, we have to contend with our own ignorance. We do not see very much. We might have a great painting, and there would be what would appear to be a smudge in the corner. Taken alone it would be meaningless, but in relation to the entire canvas it could have tremendous meaning. We see through a glass darkly, never face-to-face in this life, and we do not know what God's whole purpose is. In our finitude we cannot know. This is the answer that came to Job in the Old Testament. The whole point of the book of Job is based on the problem of evil. His conclusion is that we see too little in order to be able to make a total judgment. What may appear evil in the detail may be part of a plan beyond our ability to know.

Fourth, evil, in the sense of our mistakes, our sins, is the necessary price of freedom. God could have made us so that we never sin, but we would not be persons. We would be pawns because we would never make a decision. God apparently determined to make persons as the climax of the creation, from matter to life, to mind, to spirit. With all of our failures, we represent the highest level we know. It was intrinsic to personhood that people should make choices. All of our life is choosing, hour after hour. It is inevitable that if people are free to choose, they are free to make the wrong choices because this is part of the price of being free. We can ask ourselves which kind of world we would rather have—a world in which all was determined, or a world of freedom, pain, sorrow, anger, injustice, and sin? The determined world would have no meaning at all.

And finally, the more we stress the fact of evil and injustice, the more we are driven to believe in the life everlasting. If God is, and if God is like Christ, then God is wounded by our pain and sorrow. Since justice is not done in this life, there has to be another life in which justice is done, or else God is defeated. Think of the people burned in the great ovens of Germany during World War II. Were they worse than you or me? No, but they had an unjust outcome of their lives. If this life is all, then God's redemptive purpose is defeated, and no Christian believes that it will be defeated. Therefore, there has to be life after death to make the possibility of the occurrence of justice.

It is extremely important that professing Christians have some kind of a valid answer to give to these problems. We are at a place today where the rank and file of Christians have to be the ones who give the answers, for they are the ones who are asked the questions.

The Life We Prize

Coupled with questions about the problem of evil are questions about ethics. Fraud on the part of government officials is a frightening feature of our culture. Popular evangelists are found guilty of immoral conduct, thus making the burden of honest spiritual leaders far heavier to carry. In some areas of our society the terms chastity and fidelity are not even understood, partly because they are not mentioned. Many young people have never been taught that infidelity is a sin. Abstinence in some cases is not even presented as a live option.

We are now accustomed to reports from Wall Street of insider trading, in which the worldly wise cause financial harm to the innocent, with enormous sums being accumulated in a very short time. The most disturbing part of these stories is the evidence that the cheating occurs, with no apparent concern on the part of the perpetrators, for the fact that what they have done is immoral. They may fear being caught, but they do not appear to be fearful of doing wrong. It is as though the ethical question does not even enter into the picture at all. While most of our people are persons of integrity, the ones who cheat draw so much public attention that millions are understandably both puzzled and frightened.

Conscious of many examples of decline in civilization, we realize that, however advanced we may be in technology, we can go down, and the chief reason for decline is moral failure.

Shortly before his twenty-ninth birthday, on January 27, 1838, Abraham Lincoln produced the first expression of an idea that was destined to play an important part in his mature thinking a quarter of a century later. The theme he stated, and which had already begun to dominate his mind, concerned the American dream. Many human societies, he knew, had arisen to flourish for a while and then had disappeared. Would this also be true of the society that had arisen in "the fairest portion of the earth?" Lincoln was convinced, he said, that failure, if it should come, would come not by military aggression from the outside, but from inner decay. "At what point then is the approach of danger to be expected? I answer, 'If it ever reach us, it must spring up amongst us. It cannot come from abroad. If destruction be our lot, we must ourselves be its author and finisher. As a nation of freemen, we must live through all time, or die by suicide.'"

It was this theme of the endurance of the Republic that drew from Lincoln, on more than one occasion, his most memorable and most eloquent phrases, including two unforgettable references in the Gettysburg Address. What was being tested, he said, was "whether that nation, or any nation so conceived and so dedicated, can long endure." The theme provides a brilliant conclusion for the small masterpiece in the haunting words, "shall not perish from the earth." Almost a year earlier, in his Second Annual Message to Congress, the President had already risen to what may be his greatest height of eloquence, when, in dealing with the same theme, he said, "We shall nobly save or meanly lose the last, best hope of earth."

The American dream, as Lincoln understood it, is one of intrinsic nobility, but he knew that noble things can be lost. The words, "This too, shall pass," applied, he feared, even to the best things that persons ever produce. Certainly, he understood, they pass, if the conditions of survival are not met.

If we are wise, the concern of Abraham Lincoln, which arose early in his public life, will be our concern also. We know that, however rich our material resources may be, these, alone, are never sufficient. Many human societies have already failed, in spite of an abundance of natural resources and of material wealth. The chief buttress against failure must always reside in our spiritual resources and in the faithfulness with which we preserve them.

Our most profound danger lies in the widespread acceptance of a philosophical fallacy according to which we try to deny the existence of an objective moral order in the universe. The popular form this fallacy takes is that of ethical relativism. The ethical relativist believes that right is whatever the individual prefers. Some may prefer to cheat the government and others prefer to accept their responsibilities faithfully, but there is, if the relativist is correct, no fundamental difference. Millions, including many of our own people, really think that there is neither good nor bad but "thinking makes it so."

One consequence of such relativism is that the only remaining virtue is tolerance. You must tolerate what I do because I tolerate what you do! What people seldom realize is that such a philosophical position, if taken to its logical conclusion, would destroy the very notion of any moral standard at all. Since it is never reasonable to take a position unless we are prepared to accept whatever that position implies, it follows that, if I believe in absolute tolerance I must tolerate the action of the drug pusher who, for the sake of his own profit, gets young people hooked on habits which may ruin their lives, and which they may not be able to break as long as they live.

When dealing with the popular philosophy of relativism it is important to recognize that it has no connection with the Theory of Relativity, as supported by the late Albert Einstein. In fact Einstein consciously rejected ethical relativism and asserted his belief that there is a real right, as well as a real wrong.

The philosophy of ethical objectivity, which has meant a great deal in the preservation of an enduring civilization, received its strongest support in the thinking of Socrates, at the end of the fifth century, B.C. His most brilliant success, as shown by his student, Plato, lay in the way in which he led his opponents to positions of self-contradiction. Protagoras, who held that all moral standards are merely subjective, and that the opinions of all persons are consequently true, was forced to admit the correctness of those who claimed that he was himself in error. Subjectivism, when carefully examined, ends by undermining itself. In the great tradition of Western Philosophy, which, for the most part, follows the pattern established by Socrates, it is always recognized that, in important matters, the truth is hard to know, but this is no reason for failing to continue the search. There is one thing worse than failing to know the truth, and that is to deny that there is any truth to know!

The American dream will fade if any considerable portion of our population abandons the search for a real and objective moral order, and if it substitutes for this the dogma of mere self-interest. What is truly frightening now is the meek acceptance of the idea that self-interest provides an adequate way of life. Since it is now widely believed that each person is perfectly justified in getting all that he can for himself, the person who gives himself, without pay, to public service, is bound to be looked upon as some kind of oddity. The ridiculously high pay now received by some professional athletes is not even strange if the philosophy of self-interest is accepted.

One feature of a truly good society that has been encouraged in our civilization is that of voluntary service, wholly or partly without reference to financial gain. This valuable heritage is now threatened when the conventional questions are two: "What do I get?" and "When can I quit?" If such a philosophy of "Me-ism" ever prevails, the last best hope of earth will be already gone.

A motivation as powerful as greed cannot be balanced except by a motive equally strong or stronger. Historically, it can be demonstrated that the counterbalance motivation is not likely to be provided except by genuine religion. The love of self is so strong that it cannot be held in check except by something as powerful as the love of God. This is why a fundamental condition of endurance is spiritual vitality, without which the Republic is doomed. Most of what we do, in our effort to build a just society, is determined by the way in which we answer the fundamental question of what humans are. If each person, whatever his or her race or national origin, is really a creature made in the image of Almighty God, the practical consequences are immense.

Since all good things in human society require both constant and deliberate cultivation, we are not likely to endure, in a valuable way of life, unless we use our best thinking in dealing with the most important questions. It is the part of wisdom to realize that the dangers which we face are not primarily legal or economic ones. The basic questions thoughtful people now face are those of moral philosophy. In dealing with such questions, we must reject totally the idea that religion is a mere gloss on our culture, a decoration which may or may not be attractive. Far from being a decoration, religion provides the ground on which the edifice can be built. Are there difficulties which arise in a pluralistic society? Yes, of course there are, but these are trivial compared to the total loss of a sense of spiritual reality. We have made at least a start on meeting the conditions mentioned by Lincoln 157 years ago if we recognize that the ultimate crisis of today is a religious one.

When I wrote my book on moral philosophy, I was very careful and slow in the choice of a title. Finally I called it *The Life We Prize*. I chose this because I understood then, as I understand now, that all of us fall short of perfection. We are not always as kind or as loving as we ought to be. The life we have in mind is not the life we always demonstrate, but the life we know we *ought* to demonstrate. It is the standard that is precious and that we value supremely, because, if we lose the standard, nothing else counts.

My own life as a philosopher has been deeply influenced by the idea that ethics can be a true science. Many years ago I was fortunate in sharing, at Johns Hopkins University, in one of the famous seminars of Professor Arthur O. Lovejoy, the topic being "The Right and the Good." To watch a person as tough-minded as Professor Lovejoy in facing the central questions of human behavior was a truly rewarding experience. I determined to try to be as objective in dealing with moral questions as were my colleagues who dealt with chemistry and physics and medicine.

To a remarkable degree, there has been agreement among ethical thinkers on the preeminence of three standards of conduct: courage, fidelity, and caring. These are not the only moral standards, but loyal acceptance of them can make a permanent difference in any human society. The essence of these, in my own thinking, is as follows:

Courage. About a hundred years ago, Robert Louis Stevenson attracted thoughtful attention by asserting that courage is the primary virtue. This is true, he said, because all of the other virtues presuppose it. People who are so afraid of being unpopular that they change positions on current issues are not good persons no matter how brilliant they may be. A vivid illustration of the importance of such a question is that of the congressman who is afraid of not being re-elected. Abraham Lincoln faced such an issue and thoroughly believed that he would not be re-elected President in 1864. This belief did not cause him to change his position at all.

One of the best accounts of the meaning of courage is that of Thomas Carlyle, in his famous essay on Boswell's biography of Doctor Samuel Johnson. He perceived Johnson as a superlatively brave person, and said, in a memorable sentence, "The courage we desire and prize is not the courage to die decently, but to live manfully." Seldom in the field of literature has there been such a combination of author and subject.

Fidelity. As I go on living and learning I keep reminding myself of Johnson's famous injunction, "Clear your mind of cant." What we seek as a moral standard is truthfulness in thought and honesty in action.

Fidelity applies to both thought and action, being most obvious in the area of promises. The rule is that I must be careful in making promises, and even more careful in keeping them once they are made. It is an important feature of our culture that fidelity appears in the marriage ceremony of most of our people. "Keep thee only unto her, so long as ye both shall live," is accepted seriously by all who prize fidelity, the sanctity of marriage depending upon it.

Caring. The essence of all moral living is found, not in ourselves alone, but in our relations with other persons, for we affect the lives of others in nearly everything that we do. That is why our responsibility is not merely to have courage in ourselves, but to encourage other people. Opportunities to engage in the ministry of encouragement occur almost every day in a variety of situations, and good people are continually engaged in bearing one another's burdens. Even if I have great knowledge or great wealth, but do not care, my life is essentially a failure. So now abideth courage, fidelity, and caring, but the greatest of these is caring.

A Reasonable Place to Stand

And so, where do we stand in the wide spectrum of belief? This is a question which each of us must answer, but, in doing so, we may receive strong help from each other. Sooner or later, each person who wishes to make a difference in the thinking of the world must find or construct a platform, a reasonable faith platform on which to stand and from which to operate. As in ethics, my own involves many features but primarily three, relating to philosophy, to theology, and to the written word.

In philosophy, personalism. The most important fact we know about the universe is that, at one point in the cosmos, persons have emerged. This is not speculation, but a matter of fact. To try to understand the uniqueness of personal beings is central to any philosophy that aspires to permanence. We do not know whether there are personal beings anywhere else in the entire universe, but we do know that they exist here, and each one of us speaks from first-hand experience.

The primacy of persons came to my mind in a powerful way in 1931 when I was thirty years old. As a graduate student at Johns Hopkins University, and under the exciting influence of Professor Arthur O. Lovejoy, I was ready to choose the subject of my doctoral dissertation. For a while I thought seriously of producing something on the moral philosophy of Albert Schweitzer, and actually had a letter of agreement from the great man in Africa, but I soon switched to a broader topic, "The Uniqueness of Man." I began to ask seriously what it is that makes persons different in kind from everything else known to us in the entire universe. This was a topic highly agreeable to Professor Lovejoy.

The primacy of persons is, by any known standard, a magnificent idea. In my own thinking it was helped by the thoughts of Blaise Pascal and, even more, by the intellectual work of Max

Scheler, which was not at that time translated from the German. The primacy of persons does not mean that persons are naturally good, for they are not. There is a great deal of sin in the world, and it may be expected in any foreseeable future. What the idea of the uniqueness of persons means is that self-conscious beings can make decisions that change the course of events.

Persons differ radically from any other beings known to us. Before persons emerged there was an abundance of matter, but before the emergence of life, that was all. One of the most revolutionary ideas that have entered my mind is that a person can contemplate the universe, but the universe does not contemplate the person. Persons have bodies that are small, in comparison with many other bodies, but the minds that occupy these bodies can know and thus have real magnitude.

I am not sure when the power of this idea first struck me, but it may have come to me originally by reading the *Pensées* of Blaise Pascal. In a famous passage, Pascal said:

> Man is but a reed, the most feeble thing in nature, but he is a thinking reed. The entire universe need not arm itself to crush him. A vapor, a drop of water suffices to kill him. But if the universe were to crush him, man would still be more noble than that which killed him, because he knows that he dies and the advantage which the universe has over him; the universe knows nothing of this.

Personalism is a name I gladly adopt, because it represents the mainstream of philosophy, from the time of Socrates until now. There have been, of course, periods in which some other philosophy, such as materialism, has seemed to dominate, but it has not endured. In the recent past our academic philosophy, in the West, has sometimes decayed in that it has become little more than linguistic analysis, but there is reason to believe that this is transitory. It encourages me to see, when I visit the Harvard Yard, the bold words, "What is man that thou art mindful of him?" The greatness of such a thinker as Alfred North Whitehead will be recognized again, and the fundamental questions of human life will be addressed even after we are gone.

The philosophy of personalism, in our century, has been presented with powerful cogency by Archbishop William Temple, particularly in his famous Gifford Lectures, "Nature, Man, and God." Temple laid great stress on the idea that personalism provides a foundation for all moral philosophy, because it teaches us how to treat other people. "The principle of morality," he said, "is that we should behave as persons who are members of a Society of Persons—a Society in which personality is itself a valid claim of entrance." The practical implications of this plank in our platform are enormous. Hope lies in the effort to create a social order in which each individual, of whatever race or nationality, is recognized as being "made in God's image."

In theology, evangelicalism. I first realized that I was an evangelical Christian when I observed the influence of such a thinker as C.S. Lewis, and saw where the real power lies. As I entered more deeply into the life of the churches, both on the local and the national level, (in visits to London I saw that while many church buildings were virtually empty on Sunday mornings, the ones in which a rational evangelicalism was preached were crowded), I soon saw that the power lies neither in liberalism nor in fundamentalism, but in a Christ-centered faith. If I am asked for names to associate with this position, I find it helpful to mention the late John Baillie, long professor at the University of Edinburgh. I mention him because he was both an undoubted intellectual and also a warm-hearted follower of Jesus Christ. The recognition that this combination is possible came to me as a genuine liberation over fifty years ago.

The evangelicalism which I espouse is far removed from the position popularly associated with television evangelism, which is often marked by personal greed. This kind of evangelism sometimes seems to flourish, but, since it is not grounded in rational thought, it does not survive.

Real prayer requires a sense of being in touch with one who cares. It helped me greatly to realize not only that Christ prayed, but that his prayers were intensely personal. More and more, as I matured, I turned to Matthew 11 as the heart of the Gospel. I saw, when I realized that Christ used the pronoun "Thou", that prayer depends upon a person-to-person relation.

In literature, classicism. The greatest invention of humankind is the written word. By means of this invention we transcend both the present and the local in human experience. By employing the written word our own small lives can be enhanced as we are liberated from the merely contemporary and the merely provincial. It is our privilege both to learn from others and to use our words to teach others.

Wonderful as the invention of writing may be, not all writing is worthy of attention. At any one period in history the poor and trashy books far outnumber the valuable ones. There is far more in print than any of us can read, the consequence being that we necessarily choose. As one whose life is bound up with words, it has come to me to think how awesome is the choice of what to read and what to produce. Here is where classicism enters the picture. Why lay such stress on *The Imitation of Christ* or William Law's *Serious Call* when there are so many contemporary books that could be mentioned? The reason is now clear. The truth of any proposition is not determined by the time when it is uttered. Something first said seven hundred years ago may be far more important, and more worthy of your attention, than anything appearing in today's newspaper. The emphasis upon the contemporaneous is one of the clearest marks of the shallowness of our culture.

Classicism is our effort to guide people to the best, regardless of time. Accordingly, we need to soak our minds in the works of the acknowledged giants. A careful study of Plato's *Dialogues* may help you more in the development of a sound philosophy than can acquaintance with the works of any living author. There may be living writers whose works are as profound as Pascal's, but, if so, we certainly do not know which ones they are. There may be composers of music as brilliant as Bach, Handel, or Beethoven, but, if so, we do not know who they are. Of course we need not be ignorant of the productions of our own generation, but that is not the present danger. The present danger is that of neglect of the best that has been thought and said.

In forming your own platform watch for ways of thinking that weather the storms of changing fashion. The genuine giants, such as Socrates, Samuel Johnson, and Abraham Lincoln, outlive the changes and chances of this world. There is nothing to keep us from knowing them well.

Many years ago, while I was at Johns Hopkins University, I began to watch certain people who became my models—people of great intellectual integrity. I soon formed for myself a multiple ideal, namely that it ought to be possible to be, on the one hand, a childlike believer in the Living God—one who prays, and at the same time, one who can stand up in the symposia with the hard-thinking people who are critical of one's ideas. I said to myself, it ought to be possible to have both the warm heart, and the clear head. It ought to be possible to be both tender-hearted and tough-minded. This is the hope of all Christian theology, not only the Christian theology for clergypersons or professional theologians, but for lay Christians everywhere.

Christianity is centered, not primarily in ideas, but in events. It is based on what actually occurred, rather than on some speculation that might be pleasing. If God is truly and deeply personal, as careful thought leads us to conclude, i.e. if he can honestly be addressed as "Thou," his clearest revelation must necessarily be in the life of a person. He cannot be accurately or fully revealed in the majesty of the stars or in the terror of the storm, but he can be thus revealed in a personal life of one who knows and suffers and cares. The good news, which unites all Christians of all generations, is that such a personal revelation has occurred. It has occurred in the context of ordinary history, in the life of a person who lived at a particular time and in a particular place.

D.E.T.

CHAPTER 2

The Importance of Christ

The day was when people in theology
talked about the divinity of Christ.
Today the great strength lies in the "Christ-likeness" of God.

In our generation the shift in theology is primarily a shift in order. There was a time when in a class in theology there would always be a section about God, and then a section about Christ. The great change that we now have, in the most advanced places, begins with Christ and goes on to God. The shift begins this way: many people feel utterly confused about God—they hardly know what you mean. Many think you are talking about some kind of an abstraction, something that is beyond their conception. When they say that they believe in God, lots of them do not have the slightest idea about what the words mean.

Jesus Christ is something else. In Jesus Christ the average woman, or man, or any thinker of our time can get hold of something really concrete, historical, and understandable. Jesus Christ lived on this earth. He had a body. He lived at a known point in history, which we can locate through the various imperial regimes of the Roman Empire. We know when it was, and we know where it was; it is not something imaginary, speculative, dreamy, or on some cloud. He was a person, he lived, he suffered, he died, and he rose again.

Most Christians are familiar with the Apostles' Creed. In many congregations this is repeated over and over. The greater part of the Apostles' Creed is about Jesus Christ—about actual events in history.

He was born, he suffered, he died, and he rose. All of this is the very heart of the Creed that has held Christians together for hundreds of years. It is a center of conviction based on common belief, and it is mostly about Jesus. There is a very good reason for this spiritually. In Christ people have something that they can get hold of and, to a great measure, understand.

In our modern thinking, what then is a Christian? Because people are so confused it is terribly important to get this straight. Some people say that if you belong to this denomination, or that one, then you are a Christian. If you do not then you are not. This, however, is too narrow a view. Simply put, a Christian is a person who is committed to Christ. This is something simple enough with which to live and profound enough to change anybody's life.

The Christocentric emphasis of our generation has led to all kinds of developments. The day was when people in theology talked about the divinity of Christ. Today the great strength lies in the "Christ-likeness" of God. It means the same thing, but it is vastly more vivid to our generation. You begin with the known and you proceed by implication to the relatively unknown.

And so, a Christian is one who is committed to Jesus Christ. What does a Christian believe? He or she believes in the Christ-likeness of God. God could be just a blur. God could be cruel and vindictive. God could be a mere primal force. This is not so, if Christ is right. If Christ is right, then God is like him. You don't say he is like God, because that would assume you have a prior knowledge of what God is. You begin with what you know and proceed from there.

This logic has been one of the tremendous gains in our time. With all of our troubles, and they are numerous, ours has been a great time in Christian thought. The tremendous growth of the ecumenical spirit, the great new development in the idea of commitment, the emphasis upon renewal, all of these have been within our lifetime. And so, in many ways this is a time of genuine greatness, as well as being a time of genuine sorrow.

The Solid Point

Modern persons have searched seriously for a center of certitude: If only we can find something of which we are sure, we can go on with the business of organizing our lives. We have been strongly influenced by the beginning of modern philosophy in the words of Descartes, "I shall be entitled to entertain the highest expectations, if I am fortunate enough to discover only one thing that is certain and indubitable." But what and where is this one thing?

An important step was made in my own intellectual and spiritual career when, seventy years ago, I encountered, for the first time, the famous words of George Fox, as recorded in his *Journal*, dated 1647:

> And when all my hopes…in all men were gone, so that I had nothing outwardly to help me, nor could I tell what to do; then Oh! then I heard a voice which said, "There is one, even Christ Jesus, that can speak to thy condition; and when I heard it, my heart did leap for joy."

Today there are millions of people who have found intellectual and spiritual peace and joy by accepting something of the same faith as that described by Fox, though they have come by many different roads. The greatest vitality of the Christian community is found among persons who, though they do not claim to know very much, affirm that they believe Christ was right. A Christian is a person who bets his life that this is really so.

One result of the current emphasis on Christ as our only center of certitude is that we place great emphasis on Matthew 11:28. We believe that "rest" means a solid point. Accordingly we believe that the sentence, "Come to me, all who labor and are heavy laden and I will give you a solid point" is the heart of the gospel. Here is an idea of such transcendent importance that an entire system can be built upon it. All of the life and teaching of Jesus Christ comes to us as a consequence of a firm starting point.

One of the advantages of this approach to faith is the way in which we relate to puzzling passages of Scripture. A vivid example is that of what Scripture says about the right relation to enemies. Every honest Christian is disturbed when he or she reads, in Deuteronomy 19:21, "Your eye shall not pity, it shall be life for life, eye for eye, tooth for tooth, hand for hand, foot for foot." In short, vengeance is commanded. But everything is changed if we take seriously the Sermon on the Mount, in which Christ is recorded as saying, "You have heard that it was said, 'An eye for an eye and a tooth for a tooth.' But I say to you." Matthew 5:38,39. This brings peace of mind, for it means that Christ has made the call for vengeance obsolete. Christ-centered Christians know that they must choose and they know which to choose. The boldness of Christ in this connection is truly amazing.

Similar clarification is produced in regard to the very existence of the temple. In Christ's earthly life, there were many who saw the temple as essential for the spiritual life, but this belief Christ challenged directly. He said they were confronted with something greater than the temple. Three times, in the twelfth chapter of Matthew, he says boldly, "something greater is here."

Insofar as we are Christ-centered we are liberated from too much concern about ecclesiastical systems and organizations. The world tends to stress "princes of the church" and ceremonial clothing, but Christ does not. Far from pomp and circumstance, he says, "For the Son of Man also came not to be served but to serve." (Mark 10:45)

If we take seriously the conviction that Christ is our fulcrum, by which we are able to lift, it is important to concentrate on the life and teachings of Jesus. Few disciplines are more important than that of daily, prayerful reading of the Gospels. This is something we can never do sufficiently and we shall always make new discoveries.

Because Thomas á Kempis is honored as one of the greatest of all who have produced devotional literature, his famous advice is important: "Let our foremost resolve," he said, "be to meditate upon the Life of Jesus Christ." Christ can be accepted; he can be rejected; he cannot reasonably be ignored.

In this tremendously confused world, with so many, many voices, what do people really need? They do not need answers to every question, because they will have to work out the answers for themselves. What they need is some central point of intellectual and spiritual stability which will make them able to deal with the questions as they come, and to deal with the burdens as they are born. Christ did not say that he would take away our burdens. He did say, however, that he would give us a way of handling them.

It helped me immensely as I was studying Greek philosophy to realize that this is the significance of the famous words of a Sicilian who lived in ancient Syracuse and whose name was Archimedes. He was born in 287 B.C. and died in 212 B.C., the third century before Christ. He was one of the most famous of all thinkers in the history of the world. He made this memorable remark to the King of Syracuse. The king said, "My dear philosopher, how much can you lift?" He was talking about the fact that Archimedes had made a fulcrum. He had a lever, and he could attach the heavy weight to the short end and have many ways of manipulating the long end. I can lift 150 pounds, but he could lift a ton with no trouble. Why? Because he had a vehicle. He had a point of stability and for that we use the word "fulcrum." He must also, however, have a solid place as he operates, and so he said, "If you give me a place to stand, I can lift the whole world." If you can get far enough off it, and you had a solid fulcrum and a place to operate, the whole earth could be lifted. The deep and profound meaning of his philosophy is that the problem of lifting is not the size of the burden, but the stance of the lifting operation. That idea is tremendously profound.

As I read that, I had a great light go on in my mind. This is precisely what Jesus Christ has done for me! He has given me a fulcrum. I do not know very much. I do not know what the precise extent of the earth is. I certainly do not know the extent of the Milky Way or the whole universe. This is out of my scope. I don't need to know those things. I do know something else: I know that I trust Jesus Christ. I believe that he is trustworthy; I believe that he is dependable, and I think that if I stay with Christ I am likely to be right. In this great act of commitment I am ready to go forward and face my life, and face the day I die. The great value of this is that it gives to one a solid point. You don't need to have any more. The point is this: unless you have at least one, you are in a sea of confusion.

In Christ we have an alternative to futility, an alternative to confusion, an alternative to perplexity. Jesus saw the people, says Matthew, and he had pity on them. They were helpless and confused, wandering, like sheep without a shepherd. Of course we see that everyday of our lives. That is the story now. It was to this confusion that he was speaking when he said, come to me, all that are helpless, confused and perplexed, and I'll give you clarity and stability. Take my yoke upon you and learn of me. Become my recruit, and enter my service. Jesus did not ask for admirers, he asked for those who would commit their lives to his operation. This means that he did not claim to be just a teacher.

Many have said in our day that they respect Christ as a teacher, but not a revelation of God. They would claim that they admire some of his teachings because they recognize that he has something to say about the concern of the individual and compassion, etc. If they would think, however, they would realize that this is not adequate. If you are going to claim that Jesus was a reliable teacher, you have to pay attention to more than one kind of teaching. He did not merely teach that God loved the birds, which he did; he taught that he, himself, was the revelation of the father. "He that hath seen me," he said, "has seen the father." (John 14:9) He asserted that in his life and death, suffering and resurrection, a door was opened into the mystery of God. "No one knows the son except the father. No one knows the father except the son, and anyone to whom the son chooses to reveal him." (Matthew 11:27)

The striking thing about the teaching of Jesus was that he claimed to be more than a teacher. He was either right or wrong. If he was wrong he was a madman, making utterly absurd claims about his unique relationship to the maker of heaven and earth. If he was merely a teacher, then this was utterly absurd, something that a thoughtful person would simply reject. There is, however, another logical possibility, namely that he was telling the truth.

Historically, a Christian has been a person who believes that Christ was telling the truth, and that he wasn't just talking about flowers, birds, sheep, wayfaring men, and pathetic women. Christians believe that he was talking about the person who is at the center of the world, who will be when this world is gone, and who was before this world came into being. This is what he is saying, and it is in this that he is either right or wrong.

The important thing for a clear thinker to realize is that there is no third way. This divides the world in people's reaction to this amazing claim of Jesus Christ. He claims to tell what God is like. He claims that God cares for everyone, and that he demonstrates this himself. The glory of this is that this lifts the whole of the Christian message out of the trivial. Christianity is not just "another religion," but a conviction of a tremendous truth about the nature of God. It is no wonder that Jesus said, "I am the way, the truth, and the life. No one comes to the father but by me." (John 14:6) Absurd or gloriously true? There is no way out of facing one of those options. I have often wished that there were. As a logician, I have never been able to find a way out.

The Contribution of Christ

Belief in God. What does Christ give to all people who become committed to him? First of all, he helps us to really believe in God, because he does. He is not God; he says specifically that he is not. He says, "The father is greater than I." (John 14:28) This is unequivocal. He is not God, but he is revealing God. He is the son of God, and claims to be the door. We all know lots of reasons for believing in God; I believe in God with all my heart. I believe that God is, that God was, that God will be, and that this world is not just one of sticks and stones. It is a world that has a central purpose, and if it has a central purpose, then God has to be. The greatest practical reason for believing in God Almighty, however, is that Christ did. Either God is, or Christ is wrong. When I go through all kinds of perplexities, there is something to which I can hold. When people ask questions about my faith, I can say with complete simplicity and assuredness, "I am committed to Christ. He believed in God, so do I."

The Reality of Prayer. In consequence, commitment to Christ leads to a belief about the reality of prayer. Why? Because Christ prayed. He prayed on many occasions. In the central passage from the eleventh chapter of Matthew, the beginning is a prayer: "At that time Jesus prayed and said, 'I thank thee O Father, Lord of heaven and earth, that thou hast hid these things from the wise and understanding and hath revealed them unto babes."' (Matthew 11:25) Prayer is the direct correspondence between minds—our minds and the mind of God. I know how difficult that is to understand scientifically, but I am not baffled by those problems because Christ prayed. In my struggle to understand I say, either prayer is real or Christ was wrong.

In thinking of prayer, I turn often to the fifth chapter of I Thessalonians, concentrating on the seventeenth verse. Here I find a short sentence which answers many questions, with vivid expressions in translation of the Greek text. In the Authorized Version we say "pray without ceasing," while in the Revised Standard Version the words are "pray constantly." The translation of the New English Bible is "pray continually." The well-known translation of James Moffatt is "never give up prayer." Whichever words we employ, the idea is abundantly clear. Prayer is something in which our involvement never ends.

Prayer, rightly understood, is not an occasional effort, but a constant experience, day and night. It is reasonable, therefore, to waken from sleep in the night, and start praying. This is because there is always much for which we can pray and ought to pray. Whatever we do, or fail to do, the need is never exhausted.

Most prayer is personal. I find myself praying, "O Lord, help Mary," "O Lord, help John." The verb "help" is, almost always, central to the prayer experience, because help is what we desperately need. We pray sometimes for ourselves, but far more often we pray for others. There is strong reason to engage in intercession in that we know that it was part of the prayer life of Christ himself. In a memorable encounter we read:

> And the Lord said, Simon, Simon, behold Satan hath desired to have you, that he may sift you as wheat; But I have prayed for thee, that thy faith fail not. (Luke 22: 31-32)

One of the most important of all prayers is prayer for healing. I find, when I visit hospital patients, that vocal prayer is expected. Insofar as we take the Gospel seriously, we are bound to combine prayer with healing. There is no part of the New Testament more clear and unequivocal than that which records the stories of healing. The blind did receive their sight, the lame did walk, and the dumb did speak. Much for which Christ prayed actually occurred.

The enormous success of Alcoholics Anonymous is an important evidence of the effectiveness of prayer. Whatever they call their faith, the AA members all engage in prayer. Whether alone or with other needy persons, each AA person prays for freedom from the use of alcohol and the results are phenomenal.

Any thoughtful consideration of prayer is bound to include some reference to miracle. This is because most petitions make sense only if miracles actually occur. A miracle is not an event for which there is no cause, but one in which the will of God is clearly part of the causal sequence. In any sound philosophy there is room for both natural law and the supernatural. God, if God exists, is the author of natural law and, consequently, superior to it. Natural law, as in the case of gravitation, is God's way of producing order in the physical universe. Normally this order prevails, but it can, for an adequate reason, be transcended.

The order of the universe includes moral judgment. We are part of a world which includes not only what is, but also what ought to be. Over fifty years ago I wrote about this in a book called *The Logic of Belief*. At one point I wrote, "Good persons in all ages have interpreted their moral decisions, not in terms of something they have made, but in terms of something to which they have become sensitive."

The resurrection of Christ may be seen as an event which actually occurred, in which the moral order transcended the physical or natural order. Every prayer in which the order of events is changed, is an illustration of the supremacy of the divine will. If we realize that, in humble prayer, we are asking for the miraculous, we may have a new sense of the wonder of a life of prayer.

Again, in *The Logic of Belief*, I wrote, "If the world is really the medium of God's personal action, miracle is wholly normal. What we call a miracle is a situation in which constancy of purpose makes necessary a conspicuous adjustment of means... A miracle is an event, far from being a mysterious event, as is popularly supposed, which is really an occurrence which can be understood."

When ordinary humble persons engage in prayer, they are participating in a series of events which involve grandeur. They claim to be in contact, not merely with other finite persons, but with the Person who is at the center of the universe. They are trying to understand the purpose that is at the heart of all reality and to share in events that otherwise would not have occurred. Accordingly, the life of prayer is truly astounding.

The Life Everlasting. Some day every human body will be dead. We can say over and over with Jesus that the "night comes when no one can work." (John 9:4) Christians understand that to be true. A man who has influenced me very much had that inscribed across his watch that he carried, as a reminder. This is not, however, the end of it. The Christian is convinced that that is not the end of it. Why? Chiefly because Christ himself believed in the life everlasting, and said so, unequivocally.

Furthermore his demonstration of resurrection is of unlimited importance. I know of the confusion in the modern age. Recently I heard of three or four pastors who hate to come up to Easter day because they do not really believe in the resurrection. Those persons are not in an easy position. The truth is that the Christian movement would never have endured apart from the belief in the resurrection. The early Christians formed their witness on this belief, and of course you will find it in book after book of the New Testament.

Christianity has been the gospel of the resurrection. If it ever ceases to be it might go on as something else, but it would not be basic Christianity.

Why believe in the resurrection? Out of wish thinking? Out of our own weakness? These would not be good enough reasons. A good reason to believe in the resurrection is because of the historical evidence. Not because of what people said, but of what they became.

The facts are these: Jesus Christ was crucified, and his followers began to go away. They were utterly discouraged. Perhaps the most discouraging sentence of the New Testament is, "...we had hoped that he was the one to redeem Israel." (Luke 24:21) We had hoped. Notice the past tense. It is over now. The bubble is burst. He died just like anybody else. He claimed to be the image of the Living God, but now he is dead. And so they started back home, beaten, broken, and discouraged. One would think that that was the end. The strange thing is, however, that within a few days they were together again, strong, vibrant, and courageous. This vitality lasted not just for a night, or for a week, but for all of the rest of their lives. In spite of persecution, they said, "He arose." And the people said, "How do you know?" They said, "We have been with him." He walked with us on the way. "Did not our hearts burn within us while he talked to us on the road...?" (Luke 24:32) And the evidence, they said, was the evidence of experience.

We were not there, but we have the evidence of history, the evidence of changed lives on the part of so many. An intelligent person cannot neglect or ridicule it. Only a superficial person would try to account for it by some kind of a psychological disturbance. These were able, thoughtful, honest people, and they proved it by their lives. I don't see how anybody with a thoughtful mind can get around that. I have never heard anybody who could get around this, because this is the kind of evidence for which we have respect.

In my book, *A Place to Stand*, I wrote:

> For the Christian, Christ is not the end of the quest; he is the beginning. Starting with him, we are forced by intellectual integrity to proceed a long way. If we are committed to him, we trust him about the being and character of God, about the reality of prayer, about the possibility of miracle, and about the life everlasting. The deepest conviction of the Christian is that Christ was not wrong!

These words, written over thirty years ago, are still my conviction today. Christ is, indeed, our alternative to futility.

Somewhere in the world there should be a society consciously and deliberately devoted to the task of seeing how love can be made real and demonstrating love in practice. Unfortunately, there is really only one candidate for this task. If God, as we believe, is truly revealed in the life of Christ, the most important thing to him is the creation of centers of loving fellowship, which in turn infect the world. Whether the world can be redeemed in this way we do not know, but it is at least clear that there is no other way.

D.E.T.

CHAPTER 3

The Necessity of the Church

If one is going to be in the church, there are three requirements: to encourage one another, to be wounded by one another's sorrows, and to be elated by one another's joys.

We are surrounded today by people who believe in the adequacy of individual religion. Nothing is more common than to hear a person say, "I don't need the fellowship. I'm getting along very well. I can manage my life. I can pay my bills. I don't need the supporting fellowship." The strange thing is that this person would suppose that the main purpose for the church is merely to meet his or her needs. However strong they are is not the concern. The question is how are they going to reach others, and how are they going to build a decent society in the world?

The Christian religion differs from all others in the degree to which it is completely and integrally social. This can be seen at almost every point in the teaching of Christ. He said, "...where two or three are gathered in my name, there am I in the midst of them." (Matthew 18:20) Where is the real presence? The real presence is not in one person alone out watching the sunset, however sentimental that may be. The real presence is in the gathered community.

One Another

The early Christians began to use a phrase which accounts for much of their endurance. The two words are "one another." In I Thessalonians the phrase, "one another," appears five times. It is not a group of marbles in a bag, each separate, each unaffected by the others, each really alone, so that when they come out of the bag they are the same as when they went in. That's the mechanical conception. The early Christians moved from a mechanical conception to an organic conception—living units, which affect one another. You affect me, and I affect you. A teacher is affected by students as much as the students are affected by a teacher. A teacher does not just get up and speak into a blank space, but is watching faces, thinking of this person and his life and needs and hopes in a constant mutuality. If the teacher sees a little puzzlement on the face of a student, he or she will try to say it another way to make it clear. A person who cannot do that had better not be a teacher. A true professor is not just running off a record, but trying to make an organic experience of wholeness. This has been intrinsic in Christianity from the start.

In the patterned prayer of our Lord it is not "My Father," but "*Our* Father." "Give us this day, *our* daily bread." This was a radically different idea than most of the people of the world had ever understood, and it changed things in countless ways. It made the church a necessity. If the continuing life of Christ is to be seen chiefly in the fellowship, as he said that it is, then the church or something like it has to be formed, nurtured, and supported. I do not support the church just because I need it. I support the church because I believe there is no other way for the centrality of Christ to be made effective in the world.

The very way in which we build our meetinghouses or church buildings is a revelation. We could have buildings with a shrine. Most of the ancient Greek temples were shrines. The apostle Paul looked down into the Agora from Mars Hill and saw shrine after shrine.

These weren't meetinghouses at all, but places of individual devotion. Individual places of devotion may be a very good thing, but it isn't what Christ is talking about. His major experiences are experiences of the "group." The fact that some of the members of the group were themselves unworthy doesn't stop it at all. This is the way that the Christian faith operates.

This is the reason why Christ is reported by Luke to have prayed all night long before he chose the twelve. (Luke 6:12-13) Everything depended upon them. If they failed, all failed. How else would it have gone on if they had failed? He did not provide a second line of defense but made his own ministry vulnerable to the possible failure of the loving group. From that day to this, the church has been central. Christ spoke of "My Church," the ecclesia, the gathering. When we are in the church we are in something of terrific magnitude.

If one is going to be in the church there are three requirements: to encourage one another, to be wounded by one another's sorrows, and to be elated by one another's joys. John Donne, the dean of St. Paul's Cathedral of London, was a brilliant poet. My own introduction to him came in a very beautiful way many years ago. At Johns Hopkins University I was able to hear the poet T. S. Eliot speak most eloquently on the metaphysical poets, and the name of Donne has stayed with me. He wrote and gave a sermon that must be one of the most famous sermons of the entire world. This brilliant man in his eloquent expression said, "Every man's death diminishes me, for I am a part of mankind." I am not single and alone. If a baby is born this adds to my life. No man is an island out here alone and by itself. Every man is a part of the continent, a piece of the main. Everything that you do affects me, and everything that I do affects you. Then he made the statement for which he is best known: "Send not to ask for whom the bell tolls, it tolls for thee." Here is one of the most brilliant conceptions of the church there has ever been. We are all intertwined, and involved, we are all members one of another.

The church as we know it doesn't quite rise to that, but how good it is to get the ideal clear. The ideal is that we must never let anyone suffer alone, for every person's suffering is my pain too. We don't always live up to this, but thank God the standard is clear.

Church and Society

We don't exist as a church simply for our own self-aggrandizement, or the perfecting of our own lives, however important that might be. The church is not just a self-improvement society. We are concerned with education and its quality, or its lack of quality. We are concerned with marriage, and we are concerned with government. In essence, no part of life is exempt from our concern.

A young man came to see me, and as nearly always happens in my study, we dealt with a number of hard questions. One question we dealt with was the decay of the family in our time, which everybody knows is very real. Nobody knows how many, but there are hundreds of thousands of people, male and female, who are living together now without marriage. It is always conceivable that that would get to be the universal pattern.

The church has recognized from the beginning that it dare not let that occur. Why? Because the marriage of two people—the coming together of two people, the living together of two people affects so much more than themselves. This young man said to me, "Marriage is a wholly private affair; therefore it has nothing to do with the church. A man and a woman simply make their pledge to one another and to God and that's the end of the story." Why not just set up housekeeping and commence, claiming that it is your business, and that nobody else has a right to intrude? Many believe this to be true. I had the fortunate opportunity of showing him that there has been a continuous and impressive witness of the church of Jesus Christ to the contrary.

I thank God for the Presbyterian heritage. I have read with great care the Presbyterian discipline, and the one part which I most admire is the way in which the Presbyterian heritage utterly rejects private marriages. Why? Because the fellowship of believers is involved. We care about these people. If they have children, as they are likely to have, we must have a concern for those children, which are made in God's image, and for who Christ died. We can't just say that is none of our affair. In the characteristic Christian marriage for nearly two thousand years, the fellowship has been important. This is why we have witnesses. It isn't just their business.

Think of the hundreds of couples who have stood together in the marriage ceremony, with the man saying, "In the presence of God and before this company, I John, take thee Mary to be my wife, promising with divine assistance to be unto thee a loving and faithful husband, so long as I shall live." It lifts us all! It brings it into the whole context of the loving, worshipping, gathered community. I see no way to restore the significance and glory of marriage except by this. And who is going to do it? It isn't going to be done unless the church does it.

The same is true in the responsibility of the churches in the case of death. When a person dies, is that just a single fare so that he or she operates alone? We could just go and put the body in the ground and that could be the end of it. But Christians are called to sorrow with those who sorrow. (1 Corinthians 12:26) We must walk with the sorrowful on this long hard journey. Personally, some of the richest experiences in my life have come at a grave. I have seen the body of somebody who means a great deal to others lowered into that grave, and I know you can't just treat that like throwing away a piece of wood. Here is a person who is of unutterable value—maybe imperfect the way I'm imperfect, but of unutterable value. This person ought to be remembered by the worshipping, loving, involved community of faith. He or she is a part of the communion of saints, which is one of the most beautiful ideas in the world. In the New Testament a saint is not a good person, but a committed person, and we are trying to be that fellowship, that company of the committed. In the face of death we gather together chiefly for two purposes: one is to restate the faith, and the other is to remember the person. In a purely mechanical society, or a purely animal conception, we would not bother with either of these, but instead would just toss the person away. It is in such subtle and profound ways that the church is meant to affect society.

A Strategy of Penetration

The church, says Jesus, is meant to penetrate the world, not to hug itself to its own virtue or righteousness. It is a surprise, even to some Christians, to realize that the concept of "witness" appears both at the beginning and end of Christ's Gospel. This concept appears first in the Sermon on the Mount, soon after the Beatitudes, as the first clear commandment given to Christ's followers. After telling the little band that they were the salt of the earth (Matthew 5:13), our Lord employed another vivid metaphor by saying that they were the light of the world. No commandment is included in the reference to salt, but there is a commandment in reference to light, which is as follows, "Let your light so shine before men, that they may see your good works and give glory to your father who is in heaven." (Matthew 5:15) But this requirement to engage in public witness to the faith is not the end of the story. According to the account in the Book of Acts, the very last words of the Risen Christ reinforced the command as follows: "You shall be my witnesses in Jerusalem, and in all Judea and Samaria and to the end of the earth." (Acts 1:8)

This combination of emphasis is very impressive and provides a complete answer to those who congratulate themselves on the privacy of their faith. This is important at this time, because there are many now who take pride in the fact that they never reveal to anyone the faith by which they try to live. These people actually seem to believe that they demonstrate some kind of superior virtue by keeping to themselves whatever faith they have. Most of them do not appear to realize that they are going directly contrary to the repeated command of our Lord.

In fairness, we must try to understand the motivation of those who espouse "private religion." They do not uphold irreligion; they merely maintain that it must be kept secret, chiefly in order not to disturb anyone else. Their posture involves an appearance of virtue, in that they are trying not to invade the privacy of others. They have heard, in all probability, of some who engage in personal evangelism in truly offensive ways. Usually they are fighting something that does not occur in our generation, though it may have occurred earlier. Also, in fairness, it must be said that some people avoid the practice of witness out of real humility, believing that it is boastful to declare one's faith.

Whatever good or bad reasons there may be for upholding the doctrine of private religion, there is no doubt that the practice is contrary to the Gospel of Christ. But people are perplexed about the subject, and those who read these words must be prepared to help seekers in their perplexity. Before we can help them it is necessary to have a good understanding of the subject ourselves.

Seldom is the gospel what we would like it to be. In no respect is this more clear than in Christ's insistence upon the necessity of public witness, for witness is one of the last acts in which we hope to engage. We want to be religious, of course, but we hope to be able to practice our religion in some decently quiet and unostentatious manner. We really hope that it will not be necessary to talk about our faith at all. If possible, we avoid discussion of it in ordinary conversation, feeling far more secure if we can keep the conversation on a trivial level. The ideal is to avoid any suggestion of trying to influence others and this, we soon learn, can be done perfectly by keeping our faith as a personal and wholly private matter. This is why, "I have my own religion" is such a familiar cliché. There are some things which cultivated people do not discuss and personal faith is one of them.

We live in a period in which it is acceptable to be church members and even attendees at public worship, but great numbers who attend are careful to attend in such a way that personal involvement is kept at a minimum. That is why so many go to great lengths to try to occupy the back seats. By this means it is possible to become mere observers rather than participants. Many maintain a "balcony view," seeking thereby to be part of the audience rather than part of the cast and hoping to see rather than to be seen. "I'll come," is a common answer, "if I can slip in and out without having to do anything."

The heart of the reason for the practice of witness is the conception of sharing. It is only logical to realize that we are impelled to share anything that we prize. If a treasure is worth having, it is worth sharing. Consequently, if you refrain from passing on a conviction to others, that is good evidence that you do not truly prize it.

It is obvious that the necessity of witness is understood in all areas outside the religious realm. For example, we go to great lengths to share our political convictions. Nearly everyone who belongs to a political party works diligently to persuade outsiders of the soundness of his or her position. This is why fundraising dinners are often spectacularly successful. In the same way people are completely open about their support of athletic teams striving to increase the number of supporters. How strange it is for religious loyalty to be less powerful than secular loyalty! If, in commitment to Jesus Christ, I have found stability in my life, Christ being my only center of certitude, it is my duty to say so in the hope of thereby bringing stability into other lives.

The question of boastfulness is easily answered. When you bear unapologetic witness to Christ, you are not telling about yourself; you are telling about him. This, though it is often missed, is an important difference, when the question is raised. The person who tries to be faithful to Christ's repeated injunction by declaring his faith unapologetically is not telling who he is, but whose he is. The difference is crucial, but it is often missed.

The awful truth is that many nominal Christians are really somewhat ashamed of the faith which they are called to represent. Here is where a robust declaration of where one stands may, on occasion, be more helpful than is now realized. The golden text of those of us who understand this may be the potent words of the Apostle Paul, "I am not ashamed of the gospel." (Romans 1:16) We are imperfect people, and we are often weak when we should be strong, but all of us can belong to the Fellowship of the Unashamed.

Once we accept the central logic of the command of Christ, we need to help one another in practice in order to try to know how to perform what is commanded. The most effective witness is not that of shouting from the housetops, but the simple process of the "witness of response." By this we mean that we are often required to wait patiently for the chance to be heard. If I speak to a neighbor or to a colleague at work, and speak too soon, I may kill the thing I love, but, if I live with a person, sharing in deeds as well as words the fact that I am a really caring person, there is a good chance that the time will come when there will be a genuine sharing at the deepest level. Indeed, I must earn the right to answer, and part of the process of earning may be the process of waiting. We must let our lives speak, before our words can be heard!

The witness of response usually occurs when a troubled and perplexed person goes to another whom he has learned to trust, and says something like the following: "I have watched you operate a long time and I'd like to know what gives you the strength I have observed. What is the secret of your life? I need to know because I am facing personal problems that are too great for me to handle."

If you ever have someone come to you with words similar to the ones just stated, you are faced with a precious opportunity. This is your chance to share the deepest things in your life, wholly without fear of offense or intrusion into other lives. In such a circumstance you have no need to hold back, and the consequence may be a friendship much deeper than you have previously known.

The question of where the witness is to be made is a practical one. Some accept the erroneous idea that the proper place to engage in witness is the church fellowship. Actually this may be the place where it is least needed. Normally the best place to bear witness, both by deed and word, is the place of employment. We are called to go into all the world, and most people spend more time in the work place than anywhere else, except their own homes.

To what are we called, when Christ calls us one by one? We are called, as humble men and women, to a fellowship of sharing. We never know perfectly how to perform this calling and all of us need all of the help that we can get, but, we can begin by letting our light shine. This we do, not to glorify ourselves, but to glorify him who calls us.

The Need for Renewal

The primary reason for the decline of mainline Christianity is that it is dull. Organizations we have in abundance, with thousands of well-paid promoters, but, for the most part, nothing occurs. Dwindling numbers of persons attend weekly "services," but the lives of these attendees do not appear to be deeply affected or aroused. Many are designated by the absurd term "church goers," but what is the result of the going? The "goers" sing two or three hymns, hear someone read from the Scriptures, and listen patiently to a dull sermon. Unfortunately that is about all that occurs.

Some fresh approach to the spiritual life is clearly needed. While the faith is sound, and logically strong, we are seriously in need of new ways of nurturing it. Our central belief is that God, the one God of the whole world, is like Jesus Christ, and this belief requires no alteration, but we need new ways of handling it. We require some new handle, if the eternal truth is to be grasped.

We are helped, in this holy enterprise, by knowing, in the first place, what a true church is not. It certainly is not an organization which appears to depend upon one person for its ministry. On the whole, it must, therefore, reject the obsolete pattern of priesthood or professional religion. Professionalism in medicine is undoubtedly helpful, but the same is not true in religion. When lay people leave the cultivation of the spiritual life to one person, whom they employ and pay for this purpose, freshness tends to disappear. To expect the pastor to find the needy, to visit the homeless, and to preach all the sermons is a sure pattern for failure, because it relieves the majority of responsibility.

We shall not restore freshness unless and until we involve far more women and men in the ministry, including that of the spoken word. That the early church involved women in this kind of ministry is evident from the New Testament record, especially that of the Letter to the Church of Philippi. Not only do we know that Lydia was a true leader in the first church of Europe, we also know that the Apostle Paul mentioned other women by name. It is impressive to all who rejoice in the name of Yokefellow to realize that the very passage which employs this term for practicing Christians goes on to say, "Help these women, for they have labored side by side with me in the gospel." (Philippians 4:3)

How far removed the early church was from the limitation in the vocal ministry to one person is made clear by the description of what seems to have been a characteristic gathering, "When you come together each one has a hymn, a lesson, a revelation, a tongue, or an interpretation." (I Corinthians 14:26) Freshness was achieved, partly because Christians expected to be speakers rather than a mere audience. Bishops were not supervisors of large areas, as is now the case, but were leaders in a congregation. The use of the plural, in this connection, is surprising to contemporary readers.

When we look back into Christian history we are impressed by the way in which new life has emerged, just when the church has seemed most dead. John Wesley's work two hundred years ago is an impressive example of novelty. This appeared most of all in the formation of "class meetings," in which all present were expected to give personal testimony. The fact that most of the participants were untrained persons was no serious barrier to success. New life came surging into the entire movement! A similar phenomenon is that of the Christian Science prayer meeting, which is conducted on the simple premise that each faithful attendee is encouraged to tell his or her own story. Christian Science has succeeded, not primarily because of its theology, but because of the freshness of its method.

Limitation to particular times or places is almost sure to destroy freshness. The notion that the work of the church is limited to one hour on Sunday morning is one of the most damaging that we have encountered. Thursday may be as good a day for a living ministry as is Sunday! By reaching out to all times and places we may overcome the current staleness.

An attractive biblical figure of speech in this regard is that of re-digging the wells, the key text being Genesis 26:18, "And Isaac dug again the wells of water which had been dug in the days of his father, Abraham." The potent idea is that wells, in time, tend to become essentially useless because they are filled with silt. Unless new effort is provided, fresh water will not be available for either man or beast. The fact that the wells were satisfactory at an earlier time does not mean, we are told, that they will necessarily be satisfactory later. Because we belong to a time in which the task of re-digging is particularly required, it is our vocation to engage in re-digging!

As we seek new wineskins we soon realize that a living church, as contrasted with the conventional one, may be one which refers to secular occupations, almost every serious vocation being enriched by turning it into a ministry. A good example of this, in the recent past, is that of the Christian Legal Society. In this highly imaginative association, Christian lawyers seek to aid one another in making their daily work truly Christian. One purpose, as stated, is "to facilitate in the reconciliation of persons as well as the resolution of the dispute." Some are helped by the memorable words of Dr. Samuel Johnson, in his prayer on the study of law. The great man prayed that he might, as a consequence of his studies, be able "to prevent wrongs, and terminate contentions." If such a conception were to prevail, the court room could become as much a holy place as is any shrine.

When we apply our imaginations in the direction of vocational ministry, we soon see a multitude of new Christian opportunities. It is easy, for example, to see how Christian bankers can become ministers of money. The way in which they assist individuals and families who are in financial difficulties is wonderful to contemplate. The same goes for realtors, for land developers, and many more. Because we have long seen the application of this idea to the work of physicians and surgeons, it is not surprising that many surgeons enter the operating room in a reverential mood.

One of the truly fresh ideas of our generation is that represented by the growing number of Christian luncheon groups. At this time in my life I am deeply involved in one of these. The luncheon is limited to men who are dedicated to the ministry in daily life. We meet from exactly twelve o'clock to exactly one o'clock each Thursday noon, except for July and August, when many are on vacation. A luncheon is served by the host church women. They manage so well that they can limit the cost of each lunch to three dollars. We end precisely at one o'clock because we are aware that many of the attendees have promises to keep in the early afternoon, and we do not want to hinder them in this sacred undertaking. The speakers come from among the group itself, there being usually forty of the members thus involved in each annual season. Here we have a practical alternative to one-person religion. Normally the speaker limits himself to seventeen minutes with at least ten minutes for dialogue ensuing. We always begin and end with prayer, which is provided from within the group. We try not to show any concern about denominational affiliation. We meet in a church library that is central in location with abundant off-street parking. Though each speaker chooses his own topic, each is encouraged to make his own unapologetic witness. It is never tiresome for each one to tell how his commitment to Christ has developed in his own life, explaining the particular forms of ministry into which he has been led.

The above pattern is a very simple one, but has become spectacular in its effectiveness. Though attendance is never required, it is never a problem. For the past year we have not gone below eighty each Thursday. There are always persons present who are there for the first time, and these are cordially welcomed. Because so many of the attendees have heavy responsibilities, we understand why they cannot always be present and also why they ought not to be present. With the constant recruiting of new attendees, the absence of busy men does not become a problem. Here is a fresh pattern suitable to the needs of our time and one which may be enlarged. We are convinced that the Lord has new ways of working that we have not yet been able to understand, but that may bring fresh life in the immediate future.

In this vision of freshness, the work of faithful pastors, far from being minimized, is enlarged. Pastors are needed, not because they are called to do all of the preaching, but because they are needed to encourage lay Christians in their particular ministries. He or she is needed as the coach, stimulating and encouraging the members of the team. Of all the fresh wineskins of the contemporary church, that of pastor as coach is pre-eminent. Whenever I see a letter from a local church with stationery which says: Ministers—The Congregation; Enabler—John Jones, I am deeply encouraged.

The tragic fact is that of unrealized potential! Much of the failure to realize our potential arises from failure in expectation. We have dullness because we do not expect vitality. The task is to try to change the mood, seeking to arouse the churches to which we belong to become real fellowships, rather than passive audiences. The fact that it has actually been done anywhere is good reason to believe it can be done elsewhere. What we now seek is a change of real magnitude. We know something of the power of the original Christian fellowship as it came into the culture of the ancient Roman Empire, and how it produced tremendous change. The early Christians at Philippi, Thessalonica, and Ephesus, were not perfect people. Indeed the New Testament tells us of their sins, but, in spite of their imperfections, they really changed the world. They did, in fact, turn it upside down. (Acts 17:6)

The secret of the Christian Revolution is the reality of fellowship. The early Christians, as described in the New Testament, loved one another; they cared for one another; they supported one another; they encouraged one another. Though they were poor sticks, they, together, made a great fire. Always they knew that they followed one who said, "I came to cast a fire upon the earth." (Luke 12:49) The wonderful truth is that the consequent fire has never been extinguished. Committed Christians have the privilege of making the fire burn more brightly in the particular areas in which they live and serve.

Over thirty years ago I wrote the following on the power of small fellowships to help renew the church:

We cannot be Christians without the church, for merely individual Christianity is a contradiction in terms, but the church itself goes stale unless there are small redemptive societies which grow up within it to arouse, to stimulate and to revive. The effect that such societies have on many persons in our generation is truly phenomenal. There are grown men and women who have attended church services for years without a sense of vitality in their Christian experience, but who finally have been brought into a wholly new kind of life by meeting with a few others in a face-to-face group. Sometimes the new experience has been like a revelation. It is common for thoughtful people to report that without feeling any reality for years, the love of God is now the dominant thing in their total experience. Many, who have supposedly shared in prayer all of their lives, have suddenly discovered that power of prayer which comes when each person actually prays in a circle where there are none but participators. (*The Yoke of Christ*, p. 179.)

This is how vitality can be preserved, and how the necessity of the church can be maintained.

There is always a great temptation to stress either the inner side or the outer side of Christianity, to the exclusion of the other. Thus there are a good many people who try to set up some kind of dichotomy between what they call the social gospel and the personal gospel...I see no justification for conflict and I believe that many people in the world are looking for a religion which unites the temporal and the eternal in one miraculous whole.

D.E.T.

CHAPTER 4

A Holistic Faith

*The middle ground, equidistant from both the extreme right
and the extreme left is Rational Evangelicalism. It is evangelical
because it is Christ-centered, and it is rational because,
in the words of Socrates, it holds that every conviction
must face full examination.*

Committed Christians have a responsibility to one another, and to seekers everywhere, to present a rational set of convictions by which ordinary people can live in a time when the old denominational answers are widely discarded or forgotten. Since so many old patterns are rejected, new ones must be created. With an urgency seldom surpassed, we must try to use dedicated minds to manufacture new wineskins for the new wine. (Mark 2:22)

The Four Adjectives

The new intellectual containers of the faith must be marked by magnitude at every point. As the needs are large, so the vision must be large. For most of us this necessitates a stretching of the imagination to involve elements which we have not previously considered. In my own case I find that I must employ at least four adjectives to describe the holistic faith by which I now try to live. Consequently, when I am asked what I am, spiritually, I sometimes reply that I am a Catholic, Apostolic, Reformed, Evangelical Christian. All four of the adjectives have, historically, been employed to designate single denominations or groups of Christians, but it is easy to see that no group has a monopoly on any term or any particular conception. What each of us needs, therefore, is some way of combining features, all of which are necessary.

It is fortunate that the four words, Catholic, Apostolic, Reformed, and Evangelical have initial letters which, in combination, produce the wonderful word CARE.

Catholic: The word catholic is not the private possession of any single group of Christians, but belongs potentially to all. I try to be catholic in the sense that I want to be universal in my faith, not leaving aside any truths merely because they do not happen to be part of my own tradition. The primary opposite to catholic is sectarian. The older I become the more eager I am to avoid being sectarian, because to be sectarian is to be cut off from the main body. There have been sects in philosophy as well as religion; the chief result of them being that they have made small what ought to be large. This is the point of Dryden's statement, "No sects of old philosophers did ever leave a room for greatness."

Most of us have grown up familiar with denominations, assuming that they are normal features of the Christian faith. Consequently, when people are asked to explain themselves, they often refer to a particular denomination, which is theirs by inheritance. It is important to realize that this was not always the case. Indeed, denominations, as we know them, have not existed for more than a fourth of the Christian era. Several, with which we are familiar, are only a little more than three hundred years old, and some are far more recent than that. It is wholly possible, therefore, that denominations may be a temporary phenomena in Christian history, to be replaced by forms of organization which have not yet emerged.

The twentieth century has witnessed a strong growth in what is widely termed ecumenicity, and much of this has been good. We see, increasingly, that the true ecumenicity lies not in the rejection of one denominational heritage, but in the cherishing of others as well. Thus, if I can learn anything from Anglicans or Presbyterians or Lutherans, I hope I have the grace to receive it with gratitude. A good example of such practical Catholicism is that of the use of *The Book of Common Prayer*. This valuable compendium, which arose in the sixteenth century, is not and ought not to be the private possession of Episcopalians, but is available to anyone who can read. As a boy I never even saw *The Book of Common Prayer*, but when, as a young man, I was introduced to it, my heart leaped for joy. There is no telling how often I have turned with gratitude, to the *Collect for the Fourth Sunday after Easter*:

> O Almighty God, who alone canst order the unruly wills and affections of sinful men; Grant unto thy people, that they may love the things which thou commandest, and desire that which thou dost promise; that so, amid the sundry and manifold changes of the world, our hearts may surely there be fixed, where true joys are to be found; through Jesus Christ our Lord, Amen.

The catholic ideal which all Christians are free to espouse is that in which we do not deliberately cut ourselves off from any rich source of spiritual vitality. The way, consequently, to be truly catholic is both to learn and to share. I must be humble enough to be teachable and generous enough to share.

Apostolic: The reason why our faith must be Apostolic is that we need a firm point of reference. I need insights better than my own, and thus I find the New Testament the greatest book of the world. Something occurred, in human history, nearly two thousand years ago, and life has never been the same since that time. The Apostles were, of course, imperfect men, but they literally changed the world. This is the significance of the affirmation at Thessalonica, "These men who have turned the world upside down have come here also...."(Acts 17:6) It is no accident that, even to this day, we date all historical events as B.C. or A.D.

When the Apostle Paul went to southern Greece and, in deep turmoil of heart, sat down to write a letter to the embattled Christians of Macedonia, he could not have imagined the importance of his act. What he was doing, in fact, was to start the production of a book, including Epistles and Gospels which provided a firm basis of faith for all kinds of people, whether Jew or Gentile, whether bond or free. The fact that these remarkable literary productions came to be found together with the Hebrew Scriptures was a development of incalculable historical importance. The result was that any faith which is truly Apostolic is also biblical. We need the apostolic emphasis because it is not sufficient to be contemporary. We need roots, and the apostolic faith provides such roots in abundance. That which has no roots is bound to wither away. (Mark 4:6)

Reformed: Valuable as the ancient faith may be, and much as we honor it, we must, as Socrates taught, always engage in re-examination. "The unexamined life is not worth living." The constant need of re-examination arises from the fact that new dangers are always arising. Thus, in the Middle Ages the historic faith, in spite of its intrinsic worth, became corrupted by many harmful practices. That is why the Reformation was required. We are glad it occurred! The contribution of Martin Luther 450 years ago is one which all true Christians will always honor. If he had done nothing more than to recover the powerful idea of the "Priesthood of Every Believer," we should have abundant reason for gratitude.

The word "Reformed," which is often a synonym for "Protestant," is an excellent one. There are many spiritual dangers in "protesting," but these do not appear in "reforming." True reformers are always working for renewal, and they are humble enough to realize that, so far as each individual is concerned, it must begin with them. The movement that we term Reformation is not merely a single event of the sixteenth century, but something that, rightly understood, never ends. Just as we say, "Of his Kingdom there will be no end," (Luke 1:33) we soon realize that the same applies to the process of reform. Reformed religion will never be out of date.

Evangelical: The fourth feature of an adequate faith for our new day is that it be evangelical in the precise sense that it is Christ-centered. Evangelical is the only Christian word that is better than catholic. It is no wonder that this term has become the title of a denominational affiliation, but it is a serious mistake to suppose that its use is limited to this particular connection.

The chief reason why modern Christians must be Christ-centered is that "religion in general" turns out to be a poor thing. A merely generalized religion turns out, in practice, to be mild religion. It is mild because it lacks concreteness.

As I have already noted in Chapter 2, my own basic faith is increasingly Christ-centered, because, in Christ, I find something undeniably stable and definite. It came to me, as something of a surprise, as I meditated on the subject, that nearly all that I know about God I have learned through Christ. More and more I realize that my central conviction is that of the "Christ-likeness of God." Here my gratitude to John's Gospel is evident, because I believe the words of Christ in which he affirms that those who have seen him have, thereby, seen the father. This is strong meat, but it is only by such spiritual food that an enduring faith can be sustained.

Spirituality and Rationality

Important to my entire career has been the realization that, in many important matters, it is not necessary to choose. The fact of choice is, of course, essential to the experience of every thinking person, but it is not involved in all situations, and to know this is to know something of great practical importance. This is particularly true for a committed Christian.

Perhaps the best example of a situation in which choice is not required is that of spirituality versus rationality. The significant fact is that both of these can be treasured, and they can be held together without contradiction. The Scriptural basis for this powerful idea is found in I Corinthians 14:15, and is as follows: "I will pray with the spirit and I will pray with the mind also." In this succinct statement the Apostle Paul really settles what is for many a serious question. I can be both spiritual and intellectual, and both are needed for full vitality. The same person can engage regularly in prayer and also spend much time in thinking.

As I have noted earlier, a good example of the possibility of wholeness, with spirituality and rationality as ingredients, is that of the late John Baillie, of the University of Edinburgh. Professor Baillie was an undoubted intellectual, but he is best known as the author of *The Diary of Private Prayer*. This book, which is increasingly recognized as a genuine classic of devotion, is one of unashamed piety, but Baillie was also the author of books devoted to careful reasoning. Among those are his much admired Gifford Lectures. The reverent mood of which John Baillie was capable is well illustrated by the following sentence:

> O Thou who wast and art, and art to come, I thank thee that this Christian way wherein I walk is not an untried or uncharted road, but a road beaten hard by the footsteps of saints, apostles, prophets, and martyrs.

The scholarly, but reverent author knew, by experience, what the communion of saints can mean in practice.

In my own life, one of the most fruitful insights that have come to me has been the decision to try to combine the warm heart and the clear head, believing that these need not be in conflict at all. We live and work by faith, but it's not just any faith that will suffice. What is required is a "rational faith." It is possible to be deeply committed without being a fanatic.

In the same way it is important to understand that we do not need to choose between the "social gospel" and the "personal gospel." By the social gospel we mean that which stresses both mercy and justice, and by the personal gospel we mean that which is expressed in the life of prayer. Though these are often presented as existing in essential conflict, such is not necessarily the case. As Christians, we must try to help the poor, but, at the same time, we can pray constantly for divine guidance. One of the clearest points in the entire gospel message is the potent idea that I must love God and, at the same time, love my neighbor. (Matthew 22:37-39) To hold that a choice must be made between the two kinds of love is a heresy and a sin.

Every thoughtful person in our generation is to some extent scientifically minded. We believe in a causal system of historical events. Therefore, when there is a disease, we try to eliminate the conditions which give rise to illness, but that does not mean that we cease to pray. For my surgeon, I want to have a skilled technician, but this need not eliminate dependence upon divine power. I am glad when I learn that my physician prays before the operation begins. I believe in modern medicine, but I also believe in miracles. Most of my academic career has been devoted to a careful examination of a world view in which this combination is possible.

William James liked to speak of the radical difference between the tough-minded and the tender-minded. It is undoubtedly true that both types exist in our world, but they need not be mutually exclusive classes. The closer we come to the spirit of Christ, the more we are marked by both toughness and tenderness.

In my own life I was drawn very early to an appreciation of a model which convinced me that the combination expressed in I Corinthians 14:15 is really possible. The model which reached me most vividly was that of J. Rendel Harris whom I met first when I was a student of Woodbrooke College in Birmingham, England. The main outlines of Professor Harris' life were soon known to me. One hundred years ago he was a member of the remarkable faculty in the new university named for Johns Hopkins. I knew that Harris was a famous biblical scholar, able to employ many languages, and successful in the discovery of ancient manuscripts. I knew that, after ten years of teaching in America, he served for a year at the University of Leyden and was associated for several years with the University of Cambridge. Most of all I knew that, from 1903 to 1918, he was Director of Studies at Woodbrooke, where the students universally referred to him as "The Doctor." What I did not know until I met him in 1924 was that, in spite of all his academic prestige, he was unashamedly pious.

My admiration for Rendel Harris grew one evening when, with other students, I was in his home for a serious discussion at the end of which he knelt by his chair and prayed vocally with the simplicity of a little child. I suppose he was the first person I knew who combined perfectly keen rationality and unashamed piety. The power of this model has never left me in the sixty-plus years that have intervened. The wonder arises from the recognition that what has been is most certainly possible again. The most tough-minded can also be the most tender-minded.

Fifteen years after my recognition of Rendel Harris as a pattern of Christian behavior, I was with him again. The new connection was made possible by my position as a Fellow of Woodbrooke. I saw

Dr. Harris, for the last time, in May 1939 and felt very fortunate in the renewed contact because, in a few months, he was dead, killed by an early wartime bomb. The old man was very feeble and nearly blind, but his mind was as sharp as ever, especially when we talked of his productive career at Johns Hopkins. Though I did not reach Hopkins until Harris had been gone for fifty years, he was already a legend when I lived in Baltimore. In 1939, though I was thirty-eight years old, he called me "my dear boy," and showed genuine interest in my own life. I knew again that I was observing a living model of how the warm heart and the clear head can become joined. In subsequent years I have tried to live in such a way that I am not ashamed of piety.

The Dangers of both Right and Left

Christ's reference to the dangers of both the Right and the Left is of primary importance in understanding the Gospel. He saw dangerous tendencies on both extremes, and depicted the double danger, metaphorically, by reference to more than one leaven. The warning is as follows: "Take heed, beware of the leaven of the Pharisees and of the leaven of Herod." (Mark 8:15) The idea is that if we are aware of danger from only one side, we are always vulnerable.

Our two dangers, as committed Christians, are the leaven of literalism and the leaven of liberalism. The dangers of the Right are shown especially in reference to the Scriptures. The literalist drives him or herself into a position which allows no place for development. For instance, the literalist is bound to believe that God commands "an eye for an eye" (Leviticus 24:20), in spite of the fact that Christ, in the Sermon on the Mount, specifically rejected this unloving position. Christ's rejection is clear: "You have heard it was said, 'an eye for an eye and a tooth for a tooth,' but I say unto you." (Matthew

5:38-39) It is a shock to some to realize that Christ makes obsolete whole portions of the Hebrew Scriptures. A person who does not recognize this fact is not prepared to defend his or her faith in the modern world.

The truth is that there are no consistent literalists, no matter what they say about the topic. I do not know anyone who thinks that, because the Bible speaks of the "four corners of the earth" (Isaiah 11:12), the earth is rectangular. I do not know anyone who thinks that, because Christ said "I am the door" (John 10:9) that he is made of wood. All who think at all realize that much of the biblical language is highly metaphorical. This is one of the many reasons why a simplistic approach to Scripture is always unsatisfactory. We are required not only to read, but also to think.

In an equal fashion, the proponent of the Left is placed in an impossible position. The crucial weakness of the mere liberal is that he or she doesn't really believe in anything at all. Mere liberalism tends, almost inevitably, to become "permissiveness," which holds that tolerance is the only virtue. This is a position which no person can hold permanently, for he or she is always intolerant of the intolerant. As we mature, we begin to understand the radical difference between "freedom from" and "freedom to." Freedom is important to the Christian, but it comes at the end of a process rather than at the beginning. We learn an important lesson when we note that it is the churches which have nothing but liberalism to offer that are steadily declining in membership.

The middle ground, equidistant from both the extreme right and the extreme left is Rational Evangelicalism. It is evangelical because it is Christ-centered, and it is rational because, in the words of Socrates, it holds that every conviction must face full examination. In nearly all situations the chance of error appears most vividly at the extremes. The Christian leaders who make the greatest difference in the long run are not the extremists, but those who occupy a solid middle ground and holistic faith.

As we try to help one another to establish a reasonable middle ground regarding the authority of Scripture we can be helped by the famous translator, J.B. Phillips. Dr. Phillips, in his book, *The Ring of Truth*, showed how it is possible to maintain, with intellectual honesty, a position which recognizes the fact that the New Testament is inspired without falling into the error of inerrancy. After affirming that the New Testament is "in a quite special sense inspired," he goes on to balance his view. "It is not magical," he writes, "nor is it faultless; human beings wrote it." After rejecting both extremes Phillips goes on to establish a firm middle ground as follows: "but by something that I would not hesitate to describe as a miracle, there is a concentration upon that area of inner truth which is fundamental and ageless."

Where is it then we can safely stand? Not in verbal inerrancy and not in mere liberalism, neither of which can be defended, but in Jesus Christ. We find security, not in words, but the Word. The older I get, the more I am convinced that the closer we are to Christ, the more sure we can be of intellectual and spiritual integrity. The last word is still to be said by the Living Christ, who when he was on earth, said that he had much to reveal, but his followers were not yet ready to understand. (John 16:12) He is, I believe, still seeking to reveal the divine will, however slow we are to understand.

A Christ-centered faith exists at the middle of the spiritual spectrum, challenging both extremes. Now, late in my spiritual journey, I can do no better in trying to express such a faith than I did over thirty-five years ago, in my book, *The Company of the Committed*. At that time I wrote:

A Christian is a person who confesses that, amidst the manifold and confusing voices heard in the world, there is one voice which supremely wins his full assent, uniting all his powers, intellectual and emotional, into a single pattern of self-giving. That voice is Jesus Christ. A Christian not only believes that he was; he believes in him with all his heart and strength and mind. Christ appears to the Christian as the one stable point or fulcrum in all the relativities of history. Once the Christian has made this primary commitment he still has perplexities, but he begins to know the joy of being used for a mighty purpose, by which his little life is dignified.

The worst nightmare is not the disappearance of Christianity, but its continued existence on a low level. This is what may occur, for a while, unless a more demanding rationality emerges in the Church of Christ. The story of Christian history includes, we must admit, frequent decline, as well as advance. Because there is no known insurance against loss of devotion, this may occur even to the contemporary bands, but the good news is that, when old Christian societies die, others can arise to accept the responsibility of attack upon the world. This is how the Church of Christ operates.

D.E.T.

CHAPTER 5

The Future of Christianity

It is obvious that the church of the future,
whatever it turns out to be, will be centered
in people rather than in piles of brick and mortar.

We can never know the future wholly because we are finite. No thoughtful human being claims to be able to predict the future with any accuracy. We cannot predict the weather accurately; certainly we cannot predict spiritual events accurately. But this we can do: we can see what the present need is; we can see how things are moving and how the development is occurring, and this can give us some clear notion of direction.

I put some of this into a book with the title, *The Future of the Christian,* in which I did my level best, especially to demolish the idea that Christianity is going to die. I hear it all around me. I know how the late Lord Bertrand Russell announced the official end of the Christian faith by the end of our century. I soon saw that this could not possibly be true, and I argue on the basis of experience. The experience has been that people have been predicting the end of the Christian faith for centuries, and it has never occurred. The Christian faith has been able to weather the ridicule of the Athenian philosophers and the Roman persecution on the part of some of the worst emperors that ever lived, as well as the darkness of the Middle

Ages. There is nothing we can do at the end of our century that persons like Nero could not do.

Of course the faith will go on. I turn again and again to the words of Christ himself when he first mentioned the church according to our record of the Gospel. "The powers of death," he said, "will not be able to prevail." (Matthew 16:18) I believe that. And so I am not getting ready for the death of the Christian faith, but for its rebirth, for its renewal, for its growth and for its extension.

Of course there are places in which the Christian faith is in decay. There are churches that are closing and budgets that are decreasing. These are sad, but genuine facts. There are ways, however, in which we are rising, as well as declining. It has ever been so, and no doubt it always will be. But all of the evidence points to the fact that the Christian church will go on. I believe that with all my heart. But that does not mean it will go on as we have known it, and as it is now. Indeed, in many situations it will have to change in order to survive.

The Church of the Future

The church of the future may be markedly different from the church we now know. In fact, the church of tomorrow may differ as much from the church of today as the church of today differs from that of the time when the New Testament was being produced. We can see radical changes occurring already and we can participate in some of those changes, using the best thinking of which we are capable to help to guide development in profitable directions. It is obvious that the church of the future, whatever it turns out to be, will be centered in people rather than in piles of brick and mortar. There are four areas in which the winds of change are blowing.

First, ministry is the first clear indication of what the future emphasis is likely to be because more and more of those who join the church see themselves as Ministers of Christ. A good example of this trend is provided by the movement which calls itself the "Stephen Ministry." I had the opportunity to meet in St. Louis with 241 women and men who are involved in this strong movement and, as I watched them, I thought I was having a preview of the church of tomorrow.

In the group gathered in St. Louis, many denominations were represented, but this was clearly unimportant to those attending. Hardly anyone cared. All seemed to feel that they were living and working in the post-denominational age and they knew exactly where they wished to place the emphasis in their lives. They were conscious of serious human needs of many kinds, and they knew that each of us is surrounded by persons who are hurting in one way or another. The problem, each saw, is twofold: to be aware of the needs of their neighbors and to be prepared to help to meet as many of such needs as possible. In short, each one present saw himself or herself as a minister, learning all the time how to minister. The idea of "minister" as a verb had taken deep hold on each one I met at St. Louis.

The Stephen Ministry takes its name from the early Christian who was stoned by an angry mob, and who prayed for his persecutors, even as he was dying. He was not one of the original Apostles but, by his martyrdom, left a legacy of great significance. The legacy emphasizes ministry, both in word and deed. For the story of Stephen, see Acts 6:5-7:60.

The emphasis on ministry has been growing throughout our century and is now so well established that it is very likely to be the center of attention in coming decades. The probability is that, in the church of the future, though we shall still have weekly gatherings as we do now, these will be meetings planned to enable Christians to help one another in preparing for the ministry of each in the week. Ministry will occur wherever people are, but especially in their places of employment. Witness to fellow ministers may become accepted parts of the gatherings of Christians, as it evidently was among those of the first century of our era.

As the twentieth century nears its end, we recognize that it has been a time of unique Christian growth. The growth has not occurred in the creation of new denominations, but in new forms of ministry. There has been a tremendous increase in the number of small fellowships, many of them devoted to group prayer.

One of the most encouraging steps in spiritual growth came at the very middle of our century, on January 1, 1950, at Rock Island, Illinois. The chief speaker at a conference of the Inter-Seminary Movement was Bishop Stephen Neill who introduced to Christian parlance the phrase "the equipping ministry." Bishop Neill dealt carefully with the text, Ephesians 4:12, making sure that a comma was avoided: He pointed out that it is the "saints" i.e., "God's people," who are called to the ministry, which is not limited to "pastors and leaders." "The task of the teacher," said Neill, is to "equip ordinary Christians for the work of the ministry in daily life." One mistake of the past has been that of supposing that only professionals are "called."

When I heard Bishop Neill, on January 1, 1950, it did not occur to me that the day might come when he and I would be good friends and associates, but this is what occurred, both in Africa and at Oxford. We joined in wonderful days at the University of Nairobi, where both of us were "equippers."

The twentieth century emphasis on the "ministry" has led to the emergence of new kinds of fellowship, some of which are vocational. A good example of vocational development is the creation of the Fellowship of Christian Athletes, founded by Don McClanen when he was a high school coach in Oklahoma. Here was an idea which had never been developed before, and many lives have been changed thereby. Partly because I had spoken at some of the FCA conferences, Don McClanen enrolled in the Earlham School of

Religion at Richmond, Indiana, and later moved on to the Church of the Savior, in Washington, D.C.

In Washington, McClanen founded "The Ministry of Money." This ministry was developed chiefly by gatherings at Wellspring, a retreat center in Maryland. Consequently, more than four thousand persons have been involved, each seeing that the handling of money is a holy calling. The banker, when he or she helps a young couple to avoid borrowing too much, may be in a very real ministry.

More and more, we shall be liberated from the restrictive idea that ministry is limited to one day a week. Indeed, in the church of the future, other days of the week may prove to be quite as profitable as Sunday, so far as spiritual development is concerned. Already, those who gather in Yokefellow Luncheon groups on Wednesday or Thursday find the time spent quite as productive as any spent on Sunday. In short, we may expect a real enlargement of vision so far as days of the week are concerned.

Secondly, caring is an equally important mark of any future church worth having. As the life of our time develops, we shall prize the really loving fellowship more than anything else in our lives. If a church has fine buildings and a large budget, but is not a society in which people love one another, it is not worth the sacrifice which its survival entails.

More and more, the work of the members of the church must be to seek the welfare of fellow members as well as that of people in the world. Increasingly, the golden text becomes:"…love one another, even as I have loved you…." (John 13:34) But such love must be far more than a mere emotion. Careful thinking will need to be done if we are to know how to draw out the powers of the people whose lives touch ours, turning what is potential into something that is actual. The people whom we meet will sometimes need money but, far more often, they will need encouragement.

The church of tomorrow will become great if it exhibits something markedly in contrast to the "me-ism" of the world in general. When Christians of the future gather, each may undertake to find other poor struggling souls who need a lift in their personal lives. We shall, of course, gather to pray, but our praying will be primarily for others rather than for ourselves.

As I look back upon my own public service, I realize that one of the most significant ideas which has ever entered my mind may be the one expressed in the last paragraph of *The Company of the Committed*: "Somewhere in the world there should be a society consciously and deliberately devoted to the task of seeing how love can be made real and demonstrating love in practice. Unfortunately, there is really only one candidate for this task. If God, as we believe, is truly revealed in the life of Christ, the most important thing to him is the creation of centers of loving fellowship, which in turn infect the world. Whether the world can be redeemed in this way we do not know, but it is at least clear that there is no other way."

Thirdly, learning will become more and more important in the church, as the future develops. Indeed, even the church buildings of the future will have more the appearance of an academy than that of a temple. As the church accepts responsibility for helping people to think and thus to avoid the complete decay of culture, it will, more and more, resemble a school. In the church buildings of the future, books will be everywhere in evidence. It is clear that the study which Christ requires is something too demanding to be accomplished in forty-five minutes of Sunday School on Sunday morning.

As we grow we see more and more the importance of book service. Once only a few churches had tables of books for sale, but now nearly all of the fellowships that are really alive are engaged in book sales, doing so unapologetically. It is no longer rare to see displays of the works of such intellectual giants as Reinhold Niebuhr, John Baillie, and J.B. Phillips. The immense value of such books is that they encourage ordinary Christians in the thinking process. No longer are such books supposed to be suitable only for pastors. This development has been so valuable that it is almost sure to be adopted with increasing emphasis.

And finally, leadership, far from being minimized, will be stressed in the church of the future. Already, we see clearly that there is no conflict between the idea of the ministry of all and the special work of those both gifted and trained. The key to the solution of the problem of apparent conflict is the idea of "equipment." If all Christian business persons and physicians and mothers are called to the ministry of daily life, some must take seriously the task of training them for their sacred calling. Here is where the importance of leadership arises.

It might be supposed that the growth of responsibility of the rank and file would make the pastorate finally obsolete, but that is not the way it works out. To an amazing degree, the success or failure of a church depends on the quality of leadership that is available. The leaders of the church of the future, if they are to be successful, will not draw attention to themselves, but they will be skillful in drawing out the powers and gifts of those whom they lead.

As I think of the future of the church, I find the prospect exciting. There will, undoubtedly, be new ways of serving, which are now unknown, but will be revealed as we follow divine leading. Our conviction is that Christ is still building his Church, and that, unworthy as we are, we can be partners in this holy task.

Beyond the Holding Operation

In this world, there is no such thing as a successful holding operation. If we are not going forward, we are going backward, because, in the very nature of things, we cannot stand still. We owe this insight to Professor Alfred North Whitehead, whom, long ago,

I was pleased to know personally. He became famous, especially in his later years, for epigrams that have been widely quoted, one of the most famous being the one in which he explained why a holding operation is intrinsically impossible: "Advance or decay," he wrote, "are the only choices offered to mankind." This, he thought, is part of the very nature of our universe.

One practical illustration of this truth is provided by the airplane. When traffic is too heavy to permit landing at an airport, the approaching planes are put "on hold," but of course they are not really standing still. If the plane were to be still it would fall at once.

If we believe that Whitehead's dictum is true, and if we are committed Christians, practical steps are bound to follow. Being committed means that we must find ways in which we can help to produce growth. The committed one must take new steps, and we must help one another to know what the practical steps are.

Since a holding operation is bound to fail, we are not doing enough if we merely go on as we now are. One of the most revealing facts of our time is the evidence of decay in what has been called the Mainline Church. Standard denominations, such as Presbyterian, Methodist, Disciples, and Congregationalists, have suffered an almost unbroken decline in membership, and the powerful gatherings of laymen which so encouraged us in the fifties, are now mere memories. In characteristic church gatherings the women outnumber the men, at least two to one.

Most of the individual churches continue to exist, but their gatherings are plagued with empty seats and, in some, we do little more than go through a ritual. In the standard operation there are three hymns and a sermon, with nearly everything done by the professional clergy, while the people are primarily auditors and observers. There is often little evidence that lives are changed, and it is hard to believe that the world would be any different if the operation were omitted entirely.

Once we have become realistic and have faced honestly the failure of the holding operation, our task is to think together of ways in which beneficent change may be inaugurated. What is the next step in the Christian movement?

It is easy to see, as we try to answer this practical question, what the next step is not. For example, we do not, for the most part, need more buildings. We have a great many buildings already and many of them are not fully used. The stranger from another culture would surely notice the multiplicity of buildings devoted to religious purposes, many occupying prominent locations. Some of these are both impressive and beautiful, representing sacrificial giving on the part of millions of people. Nearly all of these enjoy freedom from taxation, thus demonstrating a practical form of governmental support. The question, however, is whether the contribution to the total civilization actually justifies such support.

All of us know that it is easier to raise money for a new building than it is to perform a justifying service in the use of such a building. But, with the obvious overbuilding of the recent past, it will be increasingly difficult to raise funds for the erection of new structures.

Another step which is not needed is more organization. This is because we already have too much. We now have a vast number of committees, commissions, and denominational offices from the local to the national level. We have councils galore, culminating in the National Council of Churches, but the critic is bound to ask what real difference these organizations actually make. They, of course, provide good salaries for numerous officials, but that is not their primary purpose.

The next step that is needed, if the holding operation is to be transcended, is a change in mood. Specifically, we must change the mood according to which the majority of Christians look upon themselves as audience. Many think that their chief responsibility is to attend, or, at most, to support. The support is primarily financial, the offering being a high point in each "service."

Now the good news is that there is a live alternative to the audience syndrome. The heart of this alternative is the notion that all Christians are called to be members of a team. It is important for the team to gather, not because they are called to listen or to observe a performance, but to participate in a movement. Indeed, the more we speak of Christianity as a "movement" the better it is, because anything which is a movement must change, and thus does not try to stand still.

It is common for good people to attend religious gatherings in a thoroughly relaxed mood. Often, we feel no more responsibility than is felt when we attend a session of the symphony orchestra. At the orchestra we can safely sit back, entirely relaxed, because the conductor will lead the operation and those who play the instruments will do their part. Unfortunately, we have developed a mood in the church according to which the pastor is really seen as the conductor. In many communities the pastor does all of the vocal praying, makes the announcements, and preaches the sermon. In fact, it is easy to point to situations in which the pastor's voice is the only one that is heard, apart from singing or responsive reading. What real difference is there between this and the orchestra?

As we try to see how the audience syndrome can be transcended, we see, again, the importance of Christ's call to commitment. He envisaged something greater than the temple and also greater than the synagogue. (Matthew 12:6) He certainly is calling us to the creation of something greater than the contemporary church in America. The notion of what is greater is clarified by the language about the team. This is the clear significance of his call to take his yoke upon us, for taking a yoke means joining a team. Here is the practical alternative to the mood of the relaxed observer.

It helps us, practically, to picture Christians as participants in an academy. We see this when we note the second part of Christ's clearest call to commitment, "And learn from me." (Matthew 11:29) Those who are members of an academy are not mere observers, but learners. They learn from one another and, as they develop, they teach one another. Each is required to work intellectually, trying to think, along with others, of the right way to live and to serve in this troubled world.

The decline of the Sunday School is one of the saddest features of contemporary Christianity. In some places it has died completely, while, in others, it is only a shadow of its former vitality. We may not be able to restore the Sunday School as it was fifty years ago, but we can create a new form of learning, suited to the needs of this age.

There are three main parts of the Christian movement, the inner life of devotion, the outer life of service, and the intellectual life of thought. At different times in human history the comparative need of these three is bound to vary. Always we need to pray, to serve, and to think, but the greatest need today is of the third of these vocations. The intellectual confusion of the population is so great and so manifest, that thinking is the primary requirement.

Here is the next step for committed Christians. We need to help people, everywhere, to think clearly. The hope today is that the church may become the Academy of Christian Learners.

How do I want to be remembered? Not primarily as a Christian scholar, but rather as a loving person. This can be the goal of every individual. If I can be remembered as a truly loving person I shall be satisfied.

D.E.T.

EPILOGUE

D. Elton Trueblood: A Tribute

D r. David Elton Trueblood, author, educator, philosopher, and theologian, endowed with special gifts and holder of many honors, bestowed unnumbered blessings upon a numerous family and countless friends. He leaves to all of us who knew him and to multitudes who never met him a rich legacy of spiritual insights, intellectual and ethical challenges, and a vision of what communities of committed men and women, faithful to God's guidance, may yet do to build a better world.

A lifelong member of the Society of Friends, Elton Trueblood's teaching, speaking, and writing influenced directly the lives of many people in many faith communities around the world. At Haverford, Guilford, Harvard, Stanford, Mount Holyoke, and Earlham he inspired thousands of students over half a century of spirited classroom teaching. His thirty-six books, clearly and simply written, captivated mass audiences rarely reached by words from academic pens.

Elton's English Quaker ancestors settled on the coast of North Carolina in 1682 at the site of the present town of Elizabeth City. In 1815 a large group of Carolina Quakers, including the Truebloods, immigrated to Washington County, Indiana. In 1869 his grandfather and other members of the family moved on to Warren County, Iowa. There, on a small farm near Indianola, Elton was born on December 12, 1900, the son of Samuel and Effie Trueblood.

Molded by the close-knit Quaker community, hard work on the family farm, encouragement from proud and supportive parents and excellent teachers, Elton Trueblood developed bookish interests and a strong student record. At William Penn College, Oskaloosa, Iowa, he won high standing as scholar, debater, and football player. After preliminary studies at Brown University and Hartford Theological Seminary, he earned the graduate degree of Bachelor of Systematic Theology at Harvard in 1926. He received his Ph.D. in philosophy from the Johns Hopkins University in 1934.

His first teaching assignments were at two Friends institutions: Guilford in North Carolina and Haverford in Pennsylvania. In 1936, largely as the result of his handling of a summer appointment as acting chaplain of Harvard, he was invited to become chaplain of Stanford. Thus, he was given a public platform and a visibility that drew him increasingly into a national ministry. Former President Herbert Hoover and his wife Lou Henry Hoover were close neighbors and friends and often attended the Quaker Meeting for Worship held monthly in the Trueblood home. (That friendship led to Elton's conducting the funeral services for both of the Hoovers, presiding over Mr. Hoover's public burial before a crowd of 75,000 on a hillside overlooking the Hoover presidential library and museum at West Branch, Iowa.)

In 1945 Elton Trueblood felt a strong calling to extend his public ministry through writing and speaking—and at the same time to serve a small, Quaker liberal arts institution. Thus, he was prompted to leave his tenured full professorship at Stanford to join the faculty of Earlham College in Richmond, Indiana, as professor of philosophy. There he quickly became a major asset in the rebuilding of the college after the impoverishing years of World War II, helping in the recruiting of both faculty and students, the shaping of new educational policies, the raising of funds, and the promoting of broader public appreciation of Earlham—and of hundreds of other church-related and independent colleges. In a much-reprinted *Reader's Digest* article, "Why I Chose a Small College," he extolled these institutions as superior places for undergraduate education, where teaching was emphasized and where close faculty-student relations could be naturally fostered.

Although the teaching of undergraduates, in courses in both philosophy and religion, remained at the center of his academic life at Earlham, his interest and influence were crucial in the implementation of the risky and controversial decision by the Earlham Board to establish the graduate programs of an Earlham School of Religion. Questions about the possibility of a Quaker seminary had been debated for almost a century, but the idea had always been discouraged as "not feasible" and rejected by some Friends as "thoroughly un-Quakerly." Meanwhile, Quaker churches of the pastoral tradition seemed increasingly to draw their ministers from the ranks of the clergy trained in other denominations, or with little formal education in religion, while the unprogrammed (or "silent") Quaker Meetings and their related outreach agencies tended to draw their leadership from among Friends and non-Friends with no theological training. Elton Trueblood was one of the few "leading Quakers" who believed that this enterprise could and should be undertaken. Happily, he lived to see the Earlham School of Religion thriving and serving all branches of the Society of Friends.

Although he served on many committees of the Society of Friends and was widely recognized as one of the most eminent Quakers of the twentieth century, Elton Trueblood was very much at home in a variety of other religious communities, was a strong advocate of ecumenical activities, and was considered by many Quakers and non-Quakers as not quite fitting the popular stereotype of the "liberal activist" Quaker. His generally strong pro-Republican political views, his friendship with such prominent Republicans as Hoover, Nixon, and Eisenhower, and his strong anti-communism caused discomfort to some of the more strongly social-activist segments of Friends. He did not like the popular stereotyping of people as "conservative" and "liberal," as he considered these terms simplistic and divisive. He believed the Society of Friends, though a small denomination, was big enough for widely divergent points of view.

He liked to say that the most important word in the language is "and." On many matters of controversy, he would insist, "We have to say both-and, not either-or." By word and action he demonstrated what some saw as contradictory beliefs and habits: liberal and conservative, traditional and innovative, compassionate and tough-minded, generous and demanding. He saw the affirmation of these combinations as being human, realistic, and honest.

From his abolitionist Quaker heritage and his own sense of moral and religious imperatives, he drew strength for vigorous opposition to racial discrimination. He was an early friend and supporter of Dr. Martin Luther King, Jr. At crucial points in the civil rights struggle he appealed directly to Presidents Eisenhower and Nixon to hold to strong stands for public policies to eliminate all forms of racial discrimination and to advance equality in human rights.

On another central Quaker testimony, pacifism, he was forthright about the importance and complexity of the issue as faced by those holding political power. He struggled openly over the personal dilemma of how an individual or a state can effectively confront challenges of violence and tyranny. He wrote and spoke eloquently against war, for international reconciliation, and in support of the rights of conscience for objectors to military service, and for those who chose military service. If a government does not successfully practice peaceful relations with its neighbors, then it will face a choice of evils in times of crisis. Thus, reluctantly, he concluded during World War II that military resistance to Hitler aggression was necessary.

Avoiding simplistic admonitions for a "back to the church" or "back to the Bible" movement, he called for the reinvigorating of religious faith as the essential force necessary to sustain the ethical, moral, and social principles on which a humane and livable society must be built. He warned against what he called "churchianity" and "vague religiosity," but he also cautioned against the overly optimistic expectations of secular social-reformism or of a too-easy social gospel.

His emphasis in his books and lectures on the importance of family life was not theoretical but a reflection of his role as husband and father. He and Pauline Goodenow, who met while they were students at William Penn College, were married in 1924. They had three sons and one daughter: Martin, born in 1925; Arnold, born in 1930; Samuel, in 1936; and Elizabeth, in 1941. They knew him throughout his life as a loving and devoted father who found ways to be available to them in spite of his heavy work responsibilities and frequent speaking trips. He consciously determined that his children should not pay a heavy price for his public career.

Tragedy struck the family in the fall of 1954 when it was discovered that Pauline was suffering from an inoperable brain tumor. The family was in the process of moving to Washington, D.C., where Elton was beginning an assignment with the U.S. Information Agency (USIA). Pauline had been a strong support and inspiration, providing needed criticism of his writings and encouraging him to fulfill his opportunities for national ministry, and managing a busy household in spite of years of chronic illness. Pauline died in early 1955.

Virginia Hodgin, a widow with two children, became Elton's secretary at Earlham in 1950 and moved to Washington to continue her work with him at the USIA. In September 1956 Elton and Virginia were married at the Washington National Cathedral, with both families in attendance. Virginia proved to be a valuable partner as well as devoted wife. With her help, he wrote and published seventeen books in the next eighteen years, ending with his autobiography, *While It Is Day*, in 1974. Virginia died in 1984.

As a writer, Elton Trueblood developed a style that emphasized clarity, conciseness, and simplicity. Among his literary mentors, of whom he spoke with the greatest sense of admiration and debt, he always listed Blaise Pascal, Dr. Samuel Johnson, Abraham Lincoln, and C.S. Lewis. He was grateful for their skill in treating serious subjects with ample use of aphorism, anecdotes, and humor. He also liked to paraphrase Mark Twain on how to get started with one's writing by saying you simply had "to glue your trousers to your chair and pick up your pen without waiting for inspiration."

To many who knew him, Elton was an almost awesome figure because of his self-discipline. To his editors at Harper and Row, he was a delight to work with, always turning in clean copy that required little editing, was delivered on or before his promised deadline, and was sure to appeal to a diverse and numerous audience. During his most productive years, he rigorously divided his day into periods of meditation, exercise, writing, and family life. Most of his books he wrote in a small cabin at the family summer home in the Pocono Mountains of Pennsylvania during the summer break in the academic year. He would contract to deliver his manuscript in early September, and begin writing on the Monday after the Fourth of July. He wrote between eight in the morning and noon, Monday through Friday, in longhand on a yellow pad. He never got personally involved with typewriters or computers!

Although his earlier books were of the longer academic type, he came to feel that any book with a serious public message, with any hope of impact on its readers, should be limited to 130 pages. He generally followed his own prescription.

Likewise, in his public speaking, he believed in being brief and to the point. His sermons and popular lectures were rarely more than twenty minutes, thirty at the outside. In classroom lectures he filled the required fifty minutes, often without a note, and ended exactly at the bell. His popularity as a public speaker was such that he could easily have devoted all his working time to the well-paying lecture circuit. Instead, he limited his speaking engagements to those audiences he wanted to reach or help, saving most of his time and energies for teaching and his family. He spoke without fee for those who could not afford to pay, but charged a standard amount for those who could.

Although he led a very busy and highly productive life, countless individuals from all walks of life remember Elton Trueblood with deep gratitude for the time he spent in private conversation with them, hearing their problems, their hopes and their dreams, and giving advice. He had extraordinary gifts in encouraging others to believe in their potential and to develop the discipline to use their gifts fully. He was a living example of the good advice he gave to others.

Landrum Bolling
January 28, 1995

A Chronology of the Life and Works of D. Elton Trueblood

No chronology can do justice to the full and rich life which the chronology seeks to highlight. This is especially so with the life of Elton Trueblood. And so, with apologies, the following is offered to show, in primitive form, the life and works of Elton Trueblood.

1900 December 12 – David Elton Trueblood is born on the family farm near Indianola, Iowa

1917 May – Elton graduates from Indianola High School

1918 September – Elton enters William Penn College, Oskaloosa, Iowa

1922 June – Elton graduates from William Penn College
August – Elton becomes pastor of Smithfield Meeting, Woonsocket, Rhode Island
September – Elton enters Brown University, Providence, Rhode Island, to study theology

1923 September – Elton enters Hartford Theological Seminary

1924 May – Elton goes to England to study at Woodbrooke College, Birmingham, and to represent American Young Friends at the 300th anniversary of George Fox's birth.
August 21 – Elton marries Pauline Goodenow at Woonsocket, Rhode Island, and moves to Boston, Massachusetts

1925   July 26 – Martin Trueblood is born in Indianola, Iowa

1926   June – Elton receives the graduate degree of Bachelor of Systematic Theology (STB) from Harvard

1927   September – The Truebloods move to Greensboro, North Carolina, where Elton becomes Assistant Professor of Philosophy and Dean of Men at Guilford College

1930   January 2 – Arnold Trueblood is born
       September – The Truebloods move to Baltimore, Maryland, for Elton to pursue a doctorate in philosophy at Johns Hopkins University. Elton is appointed Executive Secretary of Baltimore Yearly Meeting, Homewood

1931   Elton writes *Problems of Quakerism*, a group study guide for the Young Friends Movement

1933   September – The Truebloods move to the Philadelphia area where Elton joins the Haverford College faculty as Assistant Professor of Philosophy

1934   Elton writes *Studies in Quaker Pacifism* for the Philadelphia Yearly Meeting Peace Committee
       June – Elton is awarded the Doctor of Philosophy degree by Johns Hopkins University and is appointed editor of *The Friend* (Philadelphia, Pennsylvania)

1935   June – Elton is appointed interim chaplain at Harvard University for the summer session

1936   Elton writes *The Essence of Spiritual Religion*, his first full-length book
       June – The Truebloods move to Palo Alto, California, where Elton becomes chaplain and full professor at Stanford University at age 35

1938   November 29 – Elton's father, Samuel J. Trueblood, dies
       December 4 – Samuel J. Trueblood II is born

1939   Elton writes *The Knowledge of God*
        Elton is Fellow of Woodbrooke College, Birmingham,
        England, and delivers the Swarthmore Lecture at
        London Yearly Meeting. The lecture is published as *The
        Trustworthiness of Religious Experience*
1941   April 30 – Elizabeth Trueblood is born
1942   Elton writes *The Logic of Belief*
1944   Elton writes *The Predicament of Modern Man* and teaches
        at Garrett Biblical Institute for the summer and in the
        fall he teaches philosophy of religion at Harvard
1945   Elton writes *Dr. Johnson's Prayers*
1946   Elton writes *Foundations for Reconstruction*
        January to April – Elton divides his time teaching at
        Garrett Biblical Institute and Wabash College, Indiana
        April to August – Elton takes a post-war trip to
        Germany for the Friends Ambulance Unit, during which
        time he meets Landrum Bolling, future President of
        Earlham College
        September – Elton takes up teaching duties at Earlham
        College and moves the family to Richmond, Indiana
1947   Elton becomes chairman of Friends World Committee
        for Consultation (FWCC), America section
1948   Elton writes *Alternative to Futility* and becomes clerk of
        FWCC, worldwide
1949   Elton writes *The Common Ventures of Life* and begins the
        Yokefellow Movement
1950   Elton writes *Signs of Hope in a Century of Despair* and
        hears Bishop Stephen Neill speak on "The Equipping
        Ministry"
1951   Elton writes *The Life We Prize*
1952   Elton writes *Your Other Vocation* and attends the Friends
        World Conference in Oxford, England

1953   Elton writes *The Recovery of Family Life*

1954   Elton assumes position as Chief of Religious Information for the United States Information Agency (USIA) in Washington, D.C., as the family moves to Washington

1955   Elton writes *Declaration of Freedom*
February 7 – Pauline Trueblood dies

1956   Elton returns to Richmond, Indiana, and Earlham College
August 5 – Elton and Virginia Hodgin Zuttermeister are married at the National Cathedral

1957   Elton writes *Philosophy of Religion*

1958   Elton writes *The Yoke of Christ*. His study, Teague Library, is built on Earlham campus

1959   Elton writes *The Idea of a College*

1960   Elton writes *Confronting Christ*. Earlham School of Religion is founded.

1961   Elton writes *The Company of the Committed*

1963   Elton writes *General Philosophy*

1964   Elton writes *The Humor of Christ*
October – Elton conducts a graveside service for Herbert Hoover at West Branch, Iowa

1965   Elton writes *The Lord's Prayers*. The Yokefellow Institute is built on the Earlham campus

1966   Elton writes *The People Called Quakers* and retires from Earlham College to become a "professor-at-large"

1967   Elton writes *The Incendiary Fellowship* and has an extended stay in England for research and writing

1968   Elton writes *Robert Barclay: His Life and Thought*

1969   Elton writes *A Place to Stand*

1970   Elton writes *The New Man for Our Time*. He teaches at Mount Holyoke, Massachusetts

1971   Elton writes *The Future of the Christian*. Virginia Cottage, the Trueblood retirement home, is completed on the Earlham campus

1972   Elton writes *The Validity of the Christian Mission*

1973   Elton writes *Abraham Lincoln: Theologian of American Anguish*

1974   Elton writes his autobiography, *While It Is Day*

1975   Elton writes *The Meditations of Elton Trueblood*
June – Elton and Virginia visit Russia for a speaking tour at the invitation of Evangelical Christian Baptists

1977   Elton writes *Basic Christianity* and puts his energy into the Yokefellow Movement

1978   Elton writes *The Encourager* and *A Philosopher's Way*

1980   Elton writes *The Teacher*

1982   Elton writes *Essays in Gratitude*

1984   September – Virginia Trueblood dies

1988   Elton moves to Meadowood Retirement Community, Lansdale, Pennsylvania

1990   James R. Newby writes the biography *Elton Trueblood: Believer, Teacher, and Friend*

1994   March – Elton speaks before the Yokefellow Conference for the last time on the topic: "A Life of Search"
December 12 – Elton celebrates his 94th birthday
December 20 – Elton dies in his sleep
December 31 – Trueblood Memorial Service, Gwynedd, Pennsylvania

1995   January 28 – Trueblood Memorial Service, Earlham College, Richmond, Indiana

I expect to pass through this world but once. Any good, therefore, that I can do, or any kindness I can show, let me do it now. Let me not withhold or defer it, for I shall not pass this way again.

Stephen Grellet

A Life of Search
STUDY GUIDE

Elton Trueblood believed in the power of the small study group to transform lives. "One of the discoveries of the twentieth century," he wrote, "is that of the power of the small committed group. Though this was known long ago, especially among the twelve, it has been rediscovered."[6] As a result of this "discovery," Trueblood founded the Yokefellow Movement, an organization dedicated to the renewal and revitalization of the church and individual. The biblical term, Yokefellow, which is used in Philippians 4:3, is derived from Christ's call to discipleship, "Take my yoke upon you." (Matthew: 11:29) The basic pedestals on which the Yokefellow Movement are founded are four:

1. Commitment. Yokefellows hold that Christians are any persons, whether lay or clerical, who are consciously committed to Christ and to the promotion of his Kingdom.

2. Fellowship. Yokefellows recognize that a person cannot be a genuine Christian alone. To be loyal to Christ and to his cause, it is necessary to make or to find a fellowship which involves a deep sharing of life and faith. The miracle is that of the presence in the midst. (Matthew 18:20)

---

[6] Elton Trueblood, *The Small Christian Fellowship.*

3. Ministry. Yokefellows understand that a Christian is necessarily a minister. We follow one who came not to be served, but to serve. (Mark 10:45) Whatever a person's secular occupation may be, a non-ministering Christian is a contradiction in terms.

4. Discipline. If I am to be a Yokefellow I voluntarily undertake:
   a. The Discipline of Prayer. To pray every day, preferably at the beginning of the day.
   b. The Discipline of Scripture. To read reverently and thoughtfully, every day, a portion of Scripture, following a definite plan.
   c. The Discipline of Worship. To share, at least once a week, in the public worship of God.
   d. The Discipline of Money. To give a definite portion of my annual income to the promotion of Christ's cause.
   e. The Discipline of Time. To use my time as a sacred gift, not to be wasted, striving to make my daily work, whatever it may be, a Christian vocation.
   f. The Discipline of Service. To try, every day, to lift some burden.
   g. The Discipline of Study. To develop my mental powers by careful reading and study.

Hopefully the questions and prayers, which follow, and which are based upon the five chapters of this volume, will enable the committed Christian to deepen his or her own life of search. By interacting with others in a small study group, where each one trusts the other, and where the above four pedestals are foundational, the Christian seeker will be free to ask questions and gain new insights which would not be possible if confronted with these issues alone.

CHAPTER 1

A Reasonable Faith for Today

1. Do you agree with Trueblood that the Christian can "out-think" all opposition in today's world? How have your beliefs been challenged lately?

2. "All professing Christians are called to be Christian intellectuals," writes Trueblood. Do you consider yourself a "Christian intellectual?" How are you advancing your Christian intellect?

3. What are Trueblood's five responses to evil in the world? Are there ways you can share these with people who find evil a stumbling block to faith?

4. What are Trueblood's three standards of ethical conduct? How have you been challenged to practice these in your daily life?

5. What is Trueblood's three-fold platform of a reasonable faith? How does your platform agree or differ from his?

Prayer: Gracious God, grant me wisdom as I seek to understand thy will. Teach me, as a humble learner in the School of Christ, what it means to love thee with my mind, and to always be prepared to give a reason for the hope that is in me. May I be strengthened in courage, fidelity, and caring as I work to develop a reasonable faith for today. Amen.

CHAPTER 2

The Importance of Christ

1. How do you define "Christ-centered?" In what ways is this belief given expression in your daily life?

2. How do you respond to those who would say that Jesus was a good teacher, but not a revelation of God?

3. What does Trueblood believe to be the three most important contributions of Christ? Do you agree?

4. What type of historical evidence does Trueblood use to support his belief in the resurrection? Is this convincing to you?

5. "The deepest conviction of the Christian," writes Trueblood, "is that Christ was not wrong." Meditate on the words of Christ throughout the gospels. Can you hold this conviction?

Prayer: God of love and infinite wisdom, I thank thee for the life of thy son, Jesus Christ. I am grateful that amidst all of the clamoring voices and confused thought in today's world, there is one, Christ Jesus, in whom I can put my trust, and in whose teachings I have found a place to stand. Amen.

CHAPTER 3

The Necessity of the Church

1. According to Trueblood, what are the three requirements if one is going to be in the church? Does your church fellowship practice these requirements?

2. In what ways are you and your church fellowship witnessing to the world? Are you prepared to belong to what Trueblood calls the "Fellowship of the Unashamed?"

3. How is renewal being made manifest within your church fellowship? Do you believe that you are a minister regardless of profession? How so?

4. What would it take to make your church a "real fellowship" rather than a "passive audience?"

5. In the end, do you agree with Trueblood that one cannot be a Christian alone?

Prayer: Gracious God, I thank thee for the living fellowship of thy church, and for the promise of Christ that "where two or three are gathered...there I am." I pray for vitality and renewal, and that I be given strength to do my part to make the church a powerful force for good in the world. Amen.

CHAPTER 4

A Holistic Faith

1. What are the four adjectives Trueblood uses to describe the holistic faith by which he sought to live? Can you claim them as well?

2. Do you believe, with Trueblood, that this is the post-denominational age? If so, how have you experienced this personally?

3. Trueblood writes about John Baillie of the University of Edinburgh and Rendel Harris of Woodbrooke College, as models of persons who could keep spirituality and rationality in balance. Can you think of others who combine the "warm heart" and the "clear head?" How about you?

4. What does Trueblood refer to as "the double danger?" Do you agree?

5. Do you agree with Trueblood that, "A Christ-centered faith exists at the middle of the spectrum, challenging both extremes" (the Right and the Left)? How is your life of faith challenging these extremes?

Prayer: Dear God, I am grateful that I am not forced to choose between all of the various elements that comprise a holistic faith. Keep me ever sensitive to the need to maintain a balance in my life, and to understand, experientially, that the holy conjunction is *and*, and not *either/or*. Amen.

CHAPTER 5

The Future of Christianity

1. What are the four elements that Trueblood believes will mark the Church of the future, and how will they be exemplified?

2. Is your church trying to maintain a failed "holding operation?" What are the signs? What does Trueblood believe to be the "next step" if the "holding operation" is to be transcended?

3. Are you comfortable with your Christian life and the life of your church fellowship, or do you believe Christ is calling you to something greater? If so, what is this something greater?

4. What does Trueblood call the three main points of the Christian movement, and which of these does he believe needs to be stressed today? How can you help to stress this?

5. Do you believe the Christian faith has a future in this rapidly changing world? If so, in what ways are you and your church fellowship responding?

Prayer: God of the future, grant me wisdom and strength to face each day with a sense of expectancy and hope. May I be faithful to thy leading and courageous in ministry as the future unfolds. Amen.

ACKNOWLEDGMENTS
(for the 1996 edition)

Although Elton Trueblood knew that I was editing this volume, he did not live to see it completed. For this I am sorry. However, I shall be forever grateful for his life of search, and the encouragement he gave as the idea for this book moved toward reality.

Melanie Kraemer, who, until the fall of 1994, was my Administrative Assistant at the Earlham School of Religion, was kind enough not to resign from this project, and worked at home to complete it. For her meticulous eye which produced such a clean copy, I thank her.

Knowing that I would need an uninterrupted block of time to finish the work, the D. Elton Trueblood Academy Endowment Board of Directors made it possible for me to spend the month of February, 1995, on the coast of North Carolina writing and editing. It would have been impossible to complete, if not for the encouragement of Dr. Bewley Warrick, Harold Finley, Hal Owens, and Steven R. Valentine.

Finally, I thank Jarrell McCracken and Jim Todd, friends and encouragers, whose periodic telephone calls would not let the idea rest, and Karole Cox, Administrative Assistant for the Trueblood Academy who prepared the final draft of this volume for publication.

James R. Newby